THE WETWANG SAGA

THE WETWANG SAGA

The Story of Fridaythorpe, Fimber and Wetwang

*A History of England in Two
and a Half Parishes*

*Part One: From the very beginning till the end
of the Open Fields in 1806*

David Lunn

© David Lunn 2009

Published by High Wolds Heritage Publications

ISBN 978-0-9562495-0-0

Cover design by Ian Mitchell

Prepared and printed by:
York Publishing Services
64 Hallfield Road
Layerthorpe
York YO31 7ZQ
Tel: 01904 431213
www.yps-publishing.co.uk

DEDICATION

This book is dedicated first to that unknown multitude of people who have lived here in these past centuries and then to those who live here today. May God guard, guide and keep us all.

And then I must name the Venerable Bede, my fellow Geordie, who lived and worked at Jarrow and Monkwearmouth from 673 – 735. He was the first great English Scholar and his History of the English Church and People is the first great work of English History. With presumption, and some absurdity, in this work I am trying to follow in his footsteps.

ABOUT THE AUTHOR

The author – some years ago!
(but he is reading his
Venerable Bede)

David Lunn – born at Elswick, brought up at Low Fell and Cullercoats, schooled at Tynemouth – is a dedicated Geordie. Ordained in 1955 most of his ministry was in Tyneside parishes until in 1979, to his astonishment, he moved south to become Bishop of Sheffield. Since his retirement in 1997 he has lived, with great contentment, at Wetwang in the East Riding of Yorkshire.

Since his student days he has been keen on local history. At Cambridge, studying History and Theology, he researched a leaflet on his home village of Cullercoats. Whilst on the staff of Lincoln Theological College he put together short histories of each of the two tiny villages – North and South Carlton – of which, by a set of very curious chances, he had come to have pastoral care. At Sheffield he planned a series of about eight small volumes that would have covered the history of every parish in the diocese but only four had been completed when Time called a halt.

In all these modest exercises he has been as interested in the 'whys' as the 'whats' of our past history. The aim has always been to help people understand better the place in which they are living. He is now hard at work on the second part of The Wetwang Saga but is beginning to think about a big book on the whole of The High Wolds ("If I'm spared" he adds, "as my grandmother kept saying.")

CONTENTS

LIST OF ILLUSTRATIONS

THANKS

This book has been many years in gestation. It owes almost everything to a number of people who have travelled on this road before and left some record of what they had learnt. The names of many of them can be found in the Book List at the end of this book. But three people need a mention here. The Revd E Maule Cole, Vicar of Wetwang from 1865 until 1910, a skilled antiquarian and historian left us a mine of invaluable information. He was not valued by his own generation as much as he deserved. There is no memorial to him in Wetwang Church and, despite his length of service, he was never made a Canon of York Minster. Without him I doubt if this book would ever have got started. Then, fortunately today, living amongst us in the East Riding we have David and Susan Neave. Their scholarship, industry and accessibility, with the plethora of books they have written, ensures that the East Riding is the best place to be for the study, and even the writing, of local history.

That, after its long gestation, this book has come to birth, is entirely due to the High Wolds Heritage Group. Without their encouragement, technical skill and financial support it is unlikely that this book would ever have been published. My gratitude is immense. And Bill Buckle deserves a special thank you. Not only has he guided my stumbling computer skills, but has also hunted out, or taken specially, nearly all the photos in this book. Thankyou Bill.

A LETTER OF EXPLANATION

28 Southfield Road

Wetwang

25th January 2009

Dear Reader,

Yes, this is a history of Fimber, Fridaythorpe and Wetwang – but with a difference. I've tried not only to tell you most of what is known about our past but to set that into sufficient of the framework of our national history for it to make sense. I'm hopeful that this will be an interesting read to many who, though they may never have even heard of Wetwang, have an interest in the past of their own community.

The title 'The Wetwang Saga' explains itself. A 'saga', says the dictionary, is a 'heroic narrative'.

This book is the 'heroic narrative' of those who have lived and worked in this neighbourhood for the past three millennia. Nothing notably historical has ever happened in Fridaythorpe or Fimber or Wetwang and it is this that makes us special. No great name has ever lived here so this really is 'a story of ordinary country folk'. There is much talk nowadays of 'Englishness': read this book and you will begin to learn what that really is.

That there may be more in this book about church matters than you really want to know is inevitable. The archbishop of York owned Wetwang; ecclesiastical records are great survivors; the church did dominate the mediaeval world and the author, a retired bishop, can't help wrestling with the oddities of our ecclesiastical past. But if you persevere you will become a world expert in some of these matters.

Years ago, in Sermon Classes at Theological College, I was taught to 'Never under estimate the intelligence of your congregation and never over estimate their knowledge' and have stuck with this snippet of advice all my life. So if sometimes I seem to be telling you the obvious don't get angry.

This book ends about 1800. After that the new enclosed farms, the rise of the chapels, the coming of trains, new fertilisers and schools accelerate the rate of change. It is an exciting story and a group of local people have started to work together to get it all sorted and set down on paper so that they can bring you 'The Wetwang Saga Part II.' All human life will be there. It is going to be a great read.

Yours sincerely,

David Lunn

P.S Don't rush it! A paragraph or so at a time might be best.

Oddly it doesn't sound bad read aloud.

P.P.S. In a book of this complexity there are bound to be some mistakes -and certainly there are omissions. Please let me know!

Things can be put right in Part II.

THE PREFACE

The High Wolds Heritage Group aims to promote, develop and encourage a greater understanding, appreciation and enjoyment of the cultural and environmental history of the High Wolds area of Yorkshire. Towards these aims, and with the support of the Heritage Lottery Fund, one of the group's activities is the publishing of local history books. Wetwang, Fridaythorpe and Fimber are villages of the High Wolds and the High Wolds Heritage Group is delighted to be able to provide support for this book. In doing so we are meeting our aims whilst providing a good read for a wide readership.

David Lunn, since his move to the East Riding village of Wetwang, has taken an active interest in local history. He has meticulously researched the material for this book, seeking out local sources of information.

The Wetwang Saga is to be commended to anybody interested in Wetwang, Fridaythorpe and Fimber in particular, but also to anybody interested in the development of Wolds villages, in general. Throughout this well-signposted journey through the history of these villages David's personality, expecially his sense of humour, shines through. This is no dry history book but a lively description of the landscape, buildings and people living, working and dying in these High Wolds villages. This book is highly recommended to anybody interested in the history of the Yorkshire High Wolds.

David Sharpe
Chairman High Wolds Heritage Group

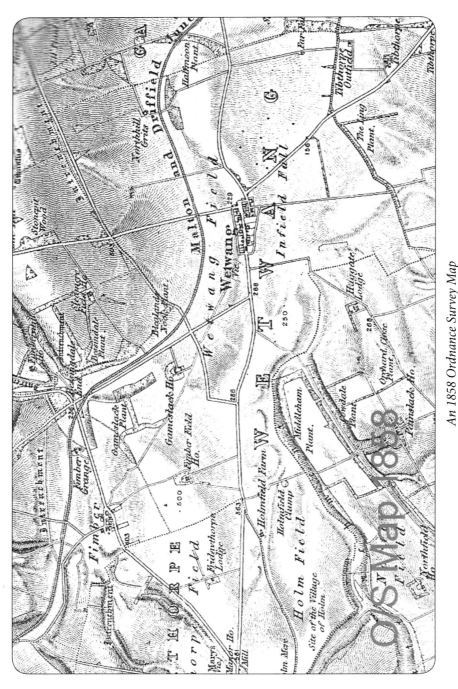

An 1858 Ordnance Survey Map

Reproduced from 2009 Ordnance Survey Map with the kind permission of the Ordnance Survey

1. LOOKING DOWN, LOOKING AROUND, AND LOOKING BACK

People have lived in and around these villages, and made their living by farming the land here for over three thousand years. And until about half a century ago very nearly everyone was involved in the daily struggle to make a living from the land by both ploughing -with oxen or horses- and keeping cattle, sheep and pigs. Surprisingly the basics of Wetwang living did not really change that much between 1000 B.C.and 1900 A.D.

But our past is, of course, much more ancient than that. The best place to begin to get some idea of Wetwang life before B.C 1000 is to stand on the Green Lane – perhaps near to the spot where it crosses the Wetwang to Sledmere Road. Here we can see nearly all the features that have been part of the environment and landscape of these villages for barely imaginable periods of time.

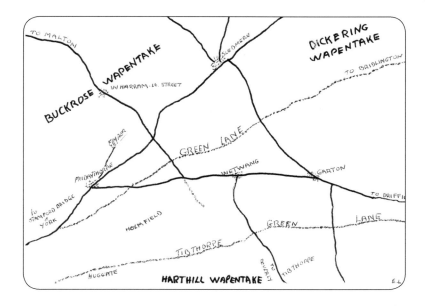

First we need to look down. We are standing on chalk -perhaps thinly covered with a rather claggy mud. This chalk, the geologists tell us, though it has been here for perhaps twenty million years, was made what it is in the eighty million years before that whilst it lay at the bottom of a mighty ocean which crushed the fishy debris into what we easily recognize as chalk -leavened somewhat mysteriously with layers and nuggets of flint. And chalk means such good drainage that rain water quickly goes underground. There are no rivers or springs in the High Wolds and until very recently all our villages were dependent on their village ponds, the rainwater that they managed to save, and the occasional very deep well for this basic necessity. But here we are on the edge of the dry Wolds: move only a mile or two down to Elmswell (Helm's springs), Kirkburn (the Church by the stream) and Little Driffield and water abounds – but not here. Rather oddly, we are in the midst of a very fertile desert.

Then look around, and having leapt through the millennia, we pause barely twenty thousand years ago at the end of the most recent Ice Age. This has given us the valley by which we stand – no river, no mountains, not much of a valley you might think. But look more carefully. Eastward we can just see how the valley opens out past Kirkburn and Driffield and then makes its way through the marshy wastes of Holderness down the River Hull to the Humber and the sea. Look west and we see the valley pointing a way into the heart of the Wolds, with Fimber on the higher ground on the far bank, till it loses itself in the multitude of tributaries that probably gives Thixendale its name of 'Sixteen Dales'. Not surprisingly this valley was the chosen route for the ambitious (foolhardy?) scheme for a railway from Driffield to Malton and the North. It was to bring coal from Newcastle to Hull. It never did. But it did get built; and struggled on for a hundred years till it quietly died in the nineteen fifties even before Dr Beeching got to work. Much of Wetwang station still stands there by the roadside in front of you.

In the centuries of melting ice, great waters flowed down this valley depositing the gravel and silt that was to make this the place where the earliest 'Wetwangers' chose to live and farm and ensures to this day that the fields before us are good strong farming land. And, most likely, this would be the time when the retreating ice left behind in some of the hollows it had made those layers of clay which made possible those ponds (or meres) that are the distinctive feature of nearly all the villages on and around the Wolds.

And now, stamping our feet on the Green Lane where we are standing, we are in touch with the earliest people who came this way. They led a semi-nomadic life moving along what soon became fixed trackways whilst finding grazing and water for themselves and their animals. Our Green Lane was one such track and even today it can be followed most of the way from Garrowby Hill to Bridlington. A similar route can be followed along the Tibthorpe Green Lane. There is something awe-inspiring about the antiquity of these trackways and the variety of people who have used them. Looking along towards the Sykes monument it is easy to imagine the Stone Age traveller bringing his precious flint axe fron flint mines at Flamborough, the 'Wetwang Princess' galloping along in her iron age 'chariot', the weary strangers from across the sea, who having made a safe landfall at the mouth of the Gypsey Race at Bridlington are now seeking out their Anglo-Saxon kith and kin newly settled on the Wolds, or, even, in a later age, the great Stage Coach from Bridlington to York trundling along this rather bumpy track as best it may. We hikers, dog-walkers, tractor drivers and motor cyclists have some very distinguished predecessors!

Then, again, we must look down and around to see the other great memorials our most distant predecessors have left behind them to astonish later ages. These are the barrows, the burial places of the ancestors, with which they made it clear that though they had no permanent settled homes this land was their land and sanctified for them by the spirits of the ancestors who lay buried at key points in their neighbourhood. Unfortunately these are not as easy to see as they once were for many have been ploughed out. And fashions in barrows can change. Way back in the New Stone Age (say 3,000 B.C.) they buried their grandest dead in huge long (and sometimes round) barrows which seem to have been the focus of an elaborate ritual landscape. One such barrow could once have been seen from here down towards Garton. We can get some idea of what it was like from its twin at Duggleby just a few miles away. Duggleby Howe is still twenty feet high (it was once ten feet higher) and two hundred feet across.

Bronze Age barrows (say after 2,000 B.C) are much more numerous. Fimber's most famous son, J.R.Mortimer, archaeologist and corn merchant, between 1860 and 1905 excavated some three hundred barrows- all within a few miles of here. Each excavation is meticulously recorded in his formidable (and curiously inaccessible) tome "Forty years' researches in British and Saxon Burial Mounds of East Yorkshire". Uniquely amongst Victorian archaeologists Mortimer, 'remarkable for the promptness and thoroughness with which he wrote up his excavations' is highly respected by the scholarly and professional archaeologists of today.

Forty of Mortimer's barrows were in front of us down in Garton Slack. ('Slack' is a Viking word for 'valley'); six were behind us up beyond the Sykes monument by Life Hill Farm; three were at Fimber and some twenty one behind us along the top of the hill behind Fimber and Towthorpe lying close to another ancient trackway. For reasons unknown to us barrow building seemed to become old-fashioned around 1500 B.C and in the past three thousand years wear and tear, and more recently, massive modern ploughs have made these ancient mounds almost invisible to the casual passer by – though some of the Towthorpe barrows still stand out against the sky line.

This plethora of stone age and bronze age barrows would alone have made this neighbourhood an archaeological paradise. But it is the changes that came gradually with the new millennium – that is after 1000 B.C- and the development of the rich and distinctive Iron Age culture as we move nearer to modern times -not much more than two thousand years ago- that enables Wetwang and its neighbourhood to put on an archaeological firework display that makes us one of the Iron Age Stars -no, THE Iron Age Star.

The Great Embankments that sometimes flank the ancient trackways, or surround ancient villages as at Fimber, or protect the heads of the valleys remain something of a mystery. They came at a time when a pattern of settled farming communities was being established and these embankments and hollow ways may have been drove ways for the vast herds of cattle that delighted Bronze Age Man. And they were certainly boundaries linked in some ways to the more ancient lines of the barrows. Sadly, it seems inevitable too, that they marked a more warlike society: the sword as well as the plough can be made from iron. Though much diminished in the last hundred years the embankments are still all around us. The most dramatic are at Huggate. Those in the woods near the Sykes Monument need only a gentle walk along the Green Lane to find them. And for those with a good landscape eye, Fimber is awash with earthworks.

Again looking down from the Green Lane into Wetwang and Garton Slack we see the site of of a huge Iron Age cemetery and village. This was exposed by the digging of gravel (which, as you can see, still goes on) and was thoroughly excavated between 1975 and 1979. With its 446 burials, two hundred small barrows and nearby Iron Age village this was not only one of the largest Iron Age cemeteries in Europe but also our prototype Wetwang. And in all the best graves there were 'chariots': chariots in Wetwang Slack, chariots by Garton Station, chariots here there and everywhere and then, astonishingly, in 2001, during an archaeological dig on the site of the ancient Manor House prior to new building, a 'chariot' emerged in the middle (nearly) of modern Wetwang. 'Chariot' is a bit misleading. The Celts – and those living around here at this time were presumably at least 'celtish'- were famous for driving into battle in chariots. (cf.Boadicea). But what we find in these burial mounds are, a shade disappointingly, more carts than chariots. And there are two further disappointments: The princess is not buried in her chariot. It had been taken to pieces and laid on top and around the body and, after 2,500 years the wood and iron has largely perished leaving only clear marks in the soil of what once was there. We cannot look at a newly excavated Iron Age chariot but we can build a very convincing replica. But all these 'chariots' do need some explanation.

The Wetwang Chariot: a reconstruction
© *Trustees of the British Museum*

Paris and the Wetwang Princess. Who were these ancient Britons building their round houses and burying their dead in Wetwang Slack? Archaeologists deal with bones and pots and they tell us nothing about the language the long-dead spoke. Historians deal with documents and books and sometimes these ancient texts can give a tongue to the people of the past. But we have no books and documents from Ancient Britain until our island begins to make some contact with the culture and empires of Greece and Rome. Julius Caesar invaded southern Britain in 56 B.C. He thought that some of the Britons had come from Gaul but those in the north had always been there. Tacitus, writing a century later, dismisses the question rather tartly: 'Who the first inhabitants of Britain were, whether natives or immigrants, remains obscure; one must remember we are dealing with barbarians.' And ancient writers are agreed that the people who lived in our East Riding were the 'Parisii' and when the Romans came and built a 'county town' for the area (near Brough on the Humber) they called it 'Civitas Parisiorum' -'The city of the Parisians.' This might be just a coincidence if it were not for the curious fact that there is another tribe called the 'Parisii' and they lived in the Seine Valley near Paris and they too buried their dead with chariots. The matter is not simplified by the odd fact that the distinctive culture of our East Riding Parisians is known as 'The Arras Culture'. But this name comes from a tiny village near Market Weighton where the first Iron Age cemetery was excavated and has nothing at all to do with France. Was there an invasion of charioteers from Gaul? The experts used to think so but most today seem to agree that the Wetangers of 300 B.C. just decided to do things differently to, and of course better than, their neighbours. Or were they just imitating the latest fashions from Paris?

Around 70 A.D the Romans came. The Parisii took this calmly and left freedom fighting to their uncouth neighbours the Brigantes. These were boom years for Wetwang with the Roman Army needing steady supplies of East Riding Oats and Barley. People have suggested that there was a Roman town here but the only traces that have been found were a series of bodies dug up where the railway crosses the Green Lane and a scattering of coins. But Burdale has turned up some significant Roman remains and there is talk of an ancient aqueduct bringing Burdale water to Fimber.

When Rome went (410 A.D) we enter the Dark Ages which means that much of what happened is guess work. We have hints of a small British kingdom of Deira covering roughly speaking the same area as the East Riding and then definite knowledge of the Anglo-Saxon Kings of Deira. Our place names show that there was a general Anglo-Saxon take over of the neighbourhood. There are many Anglo-Saxon burials along the Green Lane. And we speak Germanic English and not Celtic Welsh. But what happened to the people? Did they all flee west to safety? Or, and this is much more likely, did they just get on with the daily struggle to stay alive and if that meant learning a new language so be it.

We have spent a long time on the Green Lane digesting all this. I hope you have found it worthwhile. But I never fail to marvel when I am here (which is often with the dog) that so many thousands of years of our history is visible to us from this one spot. It is a Scottish writer, Neal Ascherson, who reminds us that 'this has been a hard country to live in, as in many ways it still is. Scottish earth is in most places – even in the more fertile south and east – a skin over bone, and like any taut face it never loses a line once acquired. Seen from the air, every trench dug over the millennia and every dyke raised, every hut footing and posthole, fort bank and cattle path, tractor mark and chariot rut seems to have inscribed its trace.' The same is true of the Wolds.

But now it is time to go down to the village to meet the Archbishop and the Danes – and turn the pages of the Domesday Book.

2. DOMESDAY BOOK AND THE DANES

THE DOMESDAY BOOK

Archaeologists can thrive with nothing but old bones and potsherds: Historians need books – or at least some scraps of ancient documents. And for the historian of Fridaythorpe and Wetwang our first book is the Domesday Book. It was in 1085 that King William, having "had much thought and very deep discussion about this country… sent his men all over England into every shire…and had a record made of how much land his archbishops had, and his bishops, and his abbots, and his earls, and what…or how much everybody had who was occupying land in England, in land or cattle and how much money it was worth…So very narrowly did he have it investigated, that there was no single hide nor a yard of land, nor indeed (it is a shame to relate but it seemed no shame to him to do) one ox nor one pig which was there left out…" That is the rather grumpy description of this first triumph of government bureaucracy by the contemporary Anglo-Saxon Chronicle. (Alas not our first newspaper but an annual record of events kept in a number of monasteries.) The work was done with astonishing speed and thoroughness and the copious returns checked, condensed and codified and bound up together in what came to be known as 'that noblest of all records' the Domesday Book. At any time this would have been an amazing administrative achievment but in a newly conquered land, with the minimal resources of the mediaeval state there is something awe-inspiring in both the ambition of this enterprise and its success. But equally amazing is both the instant authority this survey achieved and its survival to this day. You can go and see the actual documents so carefully put together nearly a thousand years ago and Penguin Books have just produced (in 2002) a magnificent and readable translation of the whole book – fourteen hundred pages of small print.

THE ROAD TO DOMESDAY

860 A.D. is not a bad starting point. By then most of what we now call England had been divided up into a number of separate Anglo-Saxon Kingdoms for over 200 years. This had not been entirely a time of peace for these kings fought each other and in turn Northumbria, then Mercia and then Wessex seemed to be top dog. But there were hardly any serious attacks from outsiders. The Britons had retreated to Wales and Strathclyde (or settled down under their new masters) and the successors to the Roman Empire on the Continent seemed to be content to leave the English to manage their own affairs.

There was a peace dividend – especially for the Church. By 700 A.D. though there were many kingdoms in 'England' there was only one Church with the leadership shared by the archbishops of Canterbury and York. And the great monasteries grew rich. In our Northumbria, for example, many of these were close to the sea – often on storm tossed headlands. Holy Island, Tynemouth, Jarrow, Monkwearmouth and Whitby can still speak to us of the faith and hopes of our Anglo-Saxon ancestors.

Then in 793 A.D., suddenly, mysterious raiders from across the sea came to the Holy Island of Lindisfarne, the most ancient and most sacred of the Northumbrian monasteries, the shrine of St Cuthbert, and destroyed it with the slaughter of most of the monks. This was the forerunner of two centuries of turmoil in which a succession of 'Viking' invaders made determined attempts first to strip the Anglo-Saxons of their wealth and then to make, if not the whole of England, at least the north of England, part of a vast 'Viking' North Sea Trading Empire. By 860 A.D. a large Danish army had defeated most of the Anglo-Saxon Kingdoms. A civil war in Northumbria did not help. In 867 the two rival kings joined forces against the common enemy and both were killed. The Danes seized York and by 876 it became clear that they had come not only to conquer but also to settle, for in that year the Anglo-Saxon Chronicle records that they 'shared out the land of the Northumbrians and they proceeded to plough and support themselves'

For much of the next two hundred years the East Riding – a Danish invention- was ruled within a Danish (and sometimes Norwegian – it is a very confused tale) kingdom based in York. And, surprisingly, since the Vikings arrived as ferociously pagan destroyers of all things Christian, the backbone of this York Viking kingdom seems to have been co-operation between a succession of kings and the archbishops of York.

In that two-hundred year journey to 1086 and the making of the Domesday Book three questions needed to find an answer: were England's rulers to be Anglo Saxons or Danes? was England to be one kingdom or many? and where was the northern frontier of that kingdom to be? We know the answers but they did not work themselves out easily. Though England had a number of Danish Kings – notably Cnut from 995-1035- geography made it likely that the Anglo Saxon royal family would prevail. The destruction of all but one of the ancient Anglo-Saxon kingdoms by the Danish invaders meant that it was the kings of that survivor -Wessex- who had the task of rebuilding Anglo-Saxon England and they saw to it that there was only going to be one England. Alfred's successors claimed to be, not kings of Wessex, but kings of all the English. Did that include Northumbria? Maybe not! By 920 the Humber had become England's northern frontier. Athelstan reigned from 924-937 and his determination to bring Northumbria under his control provoked a great alliance of Norwegians, Welsh and Scots. This he defeated in the great battle of Brunaburh (which some scholars believe took place near Kirkburn) but even this did not prevent the revival of the Norwegian kingdom of York after his death.

Stamford Bridge Memorial

The dramatic events of 1066 gave an answer to all these questions. The death of Edward the Confessor on 5th January 1066 produced the crisis. He had no heir with a compelling claim. The Duke of Normandy who had come to have an increasing influence in England claimed that the throne had been promised to him. The Norwegian king, Harold Hardrada, in alliance with rebellious Northumbrians launched an invasion through the Humber. The Anglo- Saxons choose Harold as their king. He marched north and totally defeated the Norwegians at the battle of Stamford Bridge on September 25th. Meanwhile Duke William had crossed the Channel. The Battle of Hastings followed on the 14th October and Harold was killed and his army destroyed. Duke William, now William the Conqueror, was crowned king in Westminster Abbey on Christmas Day. Quite a year 1066! It settled those three questions in an unexpected way. We had a king from the 'Northmen' – but our Danish king spoke French, had many lands in France and irrevocably pulled us away from a North Sea Empire towards continental Europe. Our national language could have become French. We had a strong king and that meant the Northumbrian claims for independence and/or links with their Scandinavian fellow-countrymen could be crushed by brute force. It wasn't done quickly. In 1069 William decided that the only way to make the north secure was to make it uninhabitable: 'In his anger he commanded that all crops and herds, chattels and food of every kind should be brought together and burned to ashes so that the whole region north of Humber might be stripped of all means of sustenance. In consequence so terrible a famine fell upon the humble and defenceless populace, that more than a 100,000 Christian folk of both sexes, young and old alike, perished of hunger.' That was written in 1114 by Orderic Vitalis, a loyal supporter of the new Norman regime, and, indeed, the evidence of the Domesday Survey supports his judgement. That Yorkshire was included in the Domesday inquiries is the conclusive proof that the Humber was no longer England's northern frontier.

OUR ENTRIES IN THE DOMESDAY BOOK

Nearly always a place name comes at least twice. For it is listed first in the account of the various landholdings -Wetwang comes under that of the archbishop of York- and then there is a summary arranged geographically – Wetwang is in Warter Hundred and Fridaythorpe, rather oddly, in that of Acklam. The summary doesn't always agree with the main entry. Is this a correction?

Wetwang's entry is very straightforward: 'In Wetwang (Wetwangham) are 13½ carucates to the geld and there could be 7 ploughs. Archbishop Ealdraed held this as 1 manor. Now Archbishop Thomas has it and it is waste. TRE (Time of King Edward ie. 1066) it was worth £4. This manor is 2 leagues long and 1½ leagues broad.'

As Fridaythorpe has always had many different owners the entries are less straightforward: Amongst the Lands of the King it is recorded 'In Fridaythorpe, Arnbiorn. 1 carucate to the geld. Land for half a plough. 5s.' Then under the Lands of the Archbishop comes 'In Fridaythorpe are 1½ carucates to the geld, of which the soke belongs to Bishop Wilton. It is waste.' Then the Land of Odo the Crossbowman includes two entries for Fridaythorpe. 'Forne and Gamal had

18 carucates of land to the geld. Land for as many ploughs. Odo has it and it is waste. TRE(1066) 20s.' (The Domesday Book, is of course handwritten and the figure '18' is uncertain) And Odo's second entry is puzzling: 'In Fridaythope are 5 carucates of land to the geld belonging to Thixendale. Inland. There is land for 5 ploughs. It is waste.'

The summary adds yet another name to the list of Landowners: 'In Fridaythorpe, the Archbishop 6 carucates and 3 bovates, The King 1 carucate, the Count of Mortain 1½ carucates, Odo the Crossbowman 7½ carucates.' Fridaythorpe is spelt variously as Fridagstorp, Fridarstorp and Fridastorp.

(Fimber, for reasons to be explored later, is not named in Domesday Book.)

WHAT DO WE LEARN FROM THE DOMESDAY BOOK?

Portrait of E.Maule Cole

First, we learn the name of the place where we live. People have lived here for thousands of years but we have no idea what they called their home village. The Danes took charge sometime after 876 and we know that they, like us, to the question "Where do you come from?" would have answered "Wetwang". Fridaythorpe probably got its name a little later but, again, for more than a thousand years, we know that Fridaythorpe has been Fridaythorpe.

Explaining names has never been an exact science. We know that 'wang' is a Scandinavian word for a field. So, not surprisingly, Ekwalls comprehensive Dictionary of English Place-Names tells us that 'Wet Wang' probably means 'wet field'. But the real experts assure us that Ekwall is wrong for Wetwang is noted for its dryness. Our chalk makes it certain that we have never had 'wet fields'. So with confidence I quote from the authoritative 'Place names of the East Riding': "There can be little doubt of the correctness of Dr Knudsen's suggestion that Wetwang is derived from the OldScandinavian legal term vaet-vangr 'field of summons' for the trial of an action." The same suggestion was powerfully and convincingly put forward by Wetwang's most distinguished

Vicar, the Revd E Maule Cole. He was Vicar from 1865 until his death in 1910. He was a noted archaeologist and antiquarian and the author of many learned articles. Stories about him, and his wife, are still told in the village. (Perhaps I should confess that I am not a 100% true believer! The idea of a 'witness field' where the legal business of a neighbourhood was regularly conducted does fit in well with what we now know about both Anglo-Saxon and Danish local government but there is just a sniff of this all being too clever to be true that leaves a niggle!)

'Fridaythorpe' is more straightforward. 'Thorpe' is Scandinavian for a new settlement developed as an off shoot from an existing community. It is tempting to think of an ambitious (or unpopular) Fridag setting out from Wetwang with his family to make his own living on the cold and stony high land outside the community limits. But Domesday's curious statement that at Fridaythorpe 'the soke belongs to Wilton' suggests that the adventurous Fridag started out from Bishop Wilton.

'Fimber' doesn't get a mention in Domesday. This might be because no one lived there in 1066. But the 'pool amidst the rough coarse grass' which gave it the name of 'Finmere' (not Fimber till 1541) would surely be there.

And Holmfield too escapes the Domesday inquisition. It might have been counted as part of Wetwang for it too belonged to the archbishops of York. There may have at some time been a chapel and a manor house (but that could have been at Holme-on-the Wolds near South Dalton) and apparently there were eight households in 1295 and eleven in 1381. Thereafter it is silence and Wetwang seems to have quietly absorbed the fields that once belonged to this Holme. Yet Holmfield still exists. A tiny signpost midway between Wetwang and Fridaythorpe points the way to the two houses that preserve the ancient name of this lost village.

Secondly, we get some idea of the size of these communities a thousand years ago. At Wetwang there are 13½ 'carucates to the geld' and at Fridaythorpe say, 16 carucates. a 'caruca' is a plough and a 'carucate' is, notionally, the area that can be ploughed with a team of eight oxen. Only in the Danish areas is the land measured in carucates. The term used everywhere else is a 'hide' and this, again notionally, is the amount of land which would support a household. So, in 1086 there was enough cultivatable ground in Wetwang for about fourteen households. The only person named in either parish in 1086 is Arnbiorn who has 1 carucate to the geld and this is described as 'land for half a plough'. This explains why though in 1086 Wetwang is pretty much derelict,

Domesday Book's scribes can confidently say that the 13½ carucates could give land for 'seven ploughs'. But the key word in all this is 'geld'. This was originally the 'danegeld' – a crisis tax to raise money to buy off the invaders. But like our Income tax, which was introduced temporarily to enable us to fight off Napoleon but soon became a permanent and indispensable basis of government finance, the geld soon became simply a regular tax on land. And though, like our council tax, it was loosely linked to the size of the property, the important figure was that in the book rather than the acres on the ground. In short the cultivatable area of both Wetwang and Fridaythorpe was much the same as it is today.

Domesday Book has two more things to teach us before we leave the rather sombre tale of 11th century Wetwang and Fridaythorpe and come to the great upturn in our fortunes that the new century would bring. One word -'waste' – makes it clear how bad things were in 1086. The experts argue at its meaning but one thing is clear: Domesday is a tax-collectors book – it tells the king where the money is. In 1066 both villages had been moderately prosperous but now at Wetwang there is nothing and at Fridaythorpe next to nothing. Has Wetwang been a desolate wilderness untouched since the slaughter – or death from hunger -of all the men women and children in that terrible harrying of the North some fifteen years earlier? That is possible. Many thousands were killed in the battle of Stamford Bridge in 1066 and we are told that many years later the bones of this multitude of horses and men still lay unburied on that gentle hillside that leads down into the village. But our own experience of war with its fearful destruction does suggest that from the darkest of nights at least glimmerings of dawn can come astonishingly quickly. Arnbiorn's single carucate at Fridaythorpe, now ploughed and worth 5s points to a better future.

And the planning of that future lay in the hands of the new owners whom the Conqueror had brought to Yorkshire. King William could be ruthless and he knew that conquest must come before reconstruction. He must have men in charge whom he could trust and who could defend his kingdom from invaders from without and rebellion within.

For Wetwang the succession is deceptively simple: in 1066 it is archbishop Eadred who owns the manor and in 1086 it is owned by his successor archbishop Thomas. For duke William had sailed from Normandy with the blessing of the Pope and certainly king William would never seize the lands of the Church. But the timely death of archbishop Eadred in 1069 (he was

Anglo-Danish and spoke the same language as the people of Wetwang) made possible the arrival of Thomas of Bayeux, a Norman-Frenchman who spoke no English. It must have been like the takeover of a sleepy family firm by a bunch of foreign entrepreneurs.

For Fridaythorpe, though the process is much more obscure, the result is the same. In 1066 the land had been shared by Forme, Gamal and the Archbishop. It seems likely that Forme and Gamal were Anglo-Danes who actually lived and worked at Fridaythorpe. They are the first of our predecessors we know by name. They should have a statue on the village green. They are replaced by Odo Arblaster (The Cross-Bowman) who has become the owner of a significant estate in a number of villages in the area. He,too, would be French-speaking. And mysteriously the Count of Mortain, William the Conqueror's half-brother and now the greatest land-owner in England has come by a small slice of Fridaythorpe. I wonder if he ever knew. There is one possible survivor from the past: the carucate owned by the King (who owned next to nothing in Yorkshire) was farmed by Arnbiorn. I like to think he may have been the son of Forme or Gamal who had come to terms with the new regime and saved something from the wreck of the family's fortunes.

3.   ARCHBISHOP THOMAS AND THE NEW WETWANG

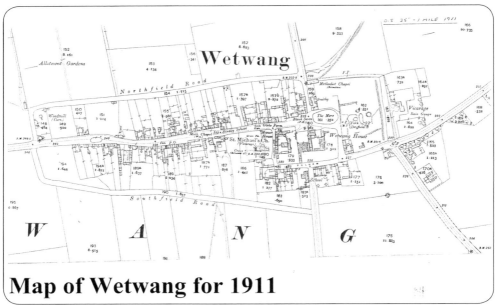

Map of Wetwang for 1911

Map of Wetwang in 1911

Wetwang is, visibly, a planned village. This may be our chief claim to fame! The farm houses and cottages are all more or less equally spaced along the main street and behind each there was (and occasionally still is) a good piece of ground backing on to the two back lanes which now have (and, surprisingly, have had for at least a hundred years,) the more grandiose names of Southfield and Northfield Road. There is a church with its burial ground at the centre of the village and a pond at each end of the main street – though one has vanished and the other is much smaller than it used to be. The village is completely encircled by the fields that have given work and food to its inhabitants. The parish boundaries, unchanging through the centuries, mark the outer edge of the fields. Nothing much of this had changed till within the living memory of some, and even now, despite the extensions southwards of Weeton Drive and Thorndale Croft and some diligent infilling the ancient plan still stands out clearly and Wetwang looks and feels like a typical English Village.

The Anglo-Saxon invaders used to be given the credit for making the change from the thousands-year-old pattern of scattered farmsteads with small fields to the central village surrounded by the open fields in shared cultivation. Excavations at Wharram Percy, and elsewhere, however, have shown that for several hundred years the Anglo-Saxons stayed with the old system and that it was only in the centuries before and after 1066 that the new planned villages became the fashion.

And when was Wetwang planned? And by whom? Almost certainly the answers are 'Before 1100' and 'Archbishop Thomas'.

At first the diocese of York had been almost coterminous with the ancient kingdom of Northumbria and had been richly endowed by that kingdom's Christian kings. By 1066 it still covered all of Yorkshire, a good bit of Lancashire and, rather oddly, Nottinghamshire as well. But so much of its wealth had been lost through the Danish invasions that it was often necessary, for financial reasons, for the archbishop of York to be bishop of Worcester as well. The last Anglo-Danish archbishop, Ealdred, though he had been a staunch supporter of King Harold, accepted William the Conqueror and indeed crowned him king in Westmister Abbey on Christmas Day 1066. He died in 1069 as the Danish Fleet was making ready yet again to sail up the Humber 'broken hearted..and praying to be spared the misery and destruction which he could see coming.' It was only after the brutal 'harrying of the North' had crushed Northumbrian insurgents and finally deterred Danish invaders that king William appointed a new archbishop, intending that he should be a key player in the reconstruction of a shattered Yorkshire. Inevitably, he came from Normandy. Thomas was from Bayeux whose bishop Odo was a half-brother of Duke William. As a close associate of the bishop he would be well known to the new king of England. He came to a scene of desolation with his cathedral in ruins, its personnel scattered or dead and his estates stolen by others or destroyed by war. Thirty years later, when he died, there had been an immense transformation: There was a huge new cathedral with a large staff of well-paid canons, his estates were in good order and no one any longer challenged Norman rule. He brought the blessings of peace to his diocese.

We can easily guess at Archbishop Thomas's Agenda:

1. Regain control of the lost estates and make them again profitable.
2. Gather together, from across Europe if necessary, a group of first-rate colleagues.
3. Build a cathedral equal to the best in Europe.
4. Restore the life of the parishes of the diocese.
5. Resist the attempts of the archbishop of Canterbury to get total ecclesiastical supremacy over the whole of England.

He was successful in the first four of these ambitions and won at least a draw in the fifth! And three of them greatly concerned Wetwang.

Wetwang had probably belonged to the archbishops of York since about 700. The Northumbrian kings had a great estate around Driffield. King Aldfrith died there in 705 (one of the best of these early kings) and is believed to be buried at Little Driffield. It seems likely that some part of this estate was given to the archbishop. This is speculation. But we know for certain that the whole of Wetwang belonged to the archbishop in 1066 and that in 1086 it was 'waste' and worth nothing. In the Middle Ages land was the only secure basis of wealth, but to release that wealth it had to be cultivated in such a way that it could feed the men who tilled it (and their families) and also produce a surplus for the landowner and, through tithe, the Church.

(Indeed the secret of a successful community in every age until modern times was a contented and industrious peasantry willing and able to grow enough to feed themselves and their families with a bit extra to keep the king, the archbishop, some soldiers and a few bureaucrats in that state of life to thich they thought they were entitled. In return 'they' would promise to maintain law and order, protect you from foreign foes, make sure that things were right with God and that you stayed alive in the best and strongest kingdom there is. The only snag, of course, is that when 'they' failed to keep their side of the bargain there was not much the poor peasant could do about it.)

Eleventh century wisdom (and probably 10th century wisdom too) said the best way forward was a centralised village with fields tilled in common and enough structure to make it responsible for its own affairs. So around 1090 the archbishop would be recruiting families from the more prosperous villages on his estates and promising them a bright future if they moved to Wetwang. The profit to the archbishop would come from his share of the harvest rather than from a cash rent. This may well have been why he built a Manor House in stone in Manor Garth. From time to time he would come and stay there (once or twice in the 13th century with the King) so that he could eat his Wetwang profits. This way of doing things was successful and continued, fundamentally unchanged, till the Enclosure Act of 1806.

Another of the archbishop's major concerns, his biographer, Hugh the Chanter writing in about 1125, tells us, was to see that his cathedral at York was staffed by 'good and reputable clerks'. I suspect that in a pan-european church with its headquarters at Rome (or Avignon) a move to distant and ruined York hardly seemed a sensible career change for an ambitious and able priest. So he 'determined to divide some of his lands which were still waste into separate prebends, to leave room for a growing number of canons; in this way each of them might be eager to build on and cultivate his own share for his own sake'. The word 'prebend' comes from the latin 'praebenda' which meant a stipend or salary. The archbishop decided to make half of his Wetwang manor one of these 'prebends'. He kept the other half for himself so that since then, though in Domesday Wetwang had been a single manor, it has always been two.

An entirely imaginary conversation will help us to understand what that first prebendary (i.e. someone who has been given a prebend) was expected to do.

Archbishop: John, I remember what a grand job you did at St Michael's in the old days when we were both in Bayeux. Now I've got a big job for you here with me at York. I want you to come to be the first prebendary of Wetwang

John: Where and what is that ? It sounds like a muddy field!

Archbishop: Nonsense. It's as dry as a bone. A lovely spot quite close to York. (Bishops whilst recruiting are usually a shade economic with the truth.) It has great possibilities. As you can imagine they've had a rough time these last few years but they are ready for a new start. I've hand picked some grand lads to go and live there and get it all going again. The soil is first class they say.

John: But what do you want me to do. I'm not into ploughing!

Archbishop: Of course not! Forget about Wetwang for now. I need you at York. It is the biggest diocese in England. I've started to build a cathedral as grand as any you have ever seen and I want you to help me make sure that the worship there is the best in the world.

And I need you to teach. Most of the clergy here can neither read nor write. How they get through the Mass I can't imagine. It is not their fault. They haven't had a chance; they need your help.

John: I like the sound of that. But what about Wetwang?

Archbishop: There are two jobs for you there. First the land there is yours -as long as you hold the prebend. You have a good head on your shoulders and it is, just in part, because I know you are a good business man that I'm asking you to take it on. Of course there will be a Steward but neither he nor any of the others will know much French and even less Latin. It would be good if you could learn a little of their language. It will make it harder for them to cheat you. But, of course the other job there is the important one. You will be the rector with the cure of souls of Wetwang and of the small village nearby -Fridaythorpe I think – as well. Wetwang has belonged to the archbishop since ancient times but you will almost be starting from scratch. You will need to build a church -or perhaps two.

John: That sounds a big job. I'd need help and I can see the language being a problem.

Archbishop: Of course. You'd probably need a Chaplain in each village. And I will need you a good deal with me. I don't want you spending too much time tramping from mud hut to mud hut in Wetwang.

John: I don't like to ask, but what about the pay ? How much is this Wetwang Prebend likely to be worth?

Archbishop: Honestly, I have to say I don't know. One day I'm sure it will be worth a great deal. It is good land and, of course as rector you will get the tithes from my Wetwang Manor as well as yours and then there is Fridaythorpe. And it is not like Normandy. That tenth of the produce to the Church has been compulsory in England for hundreds of years. They may have got a bit slack but I will see to it that it is paid. But it might be a bit tight at first. And I can't help much. I've done what I can in giving you the land. I'm getting them taught how to quarry stone. But building cathedrals doesn't come cheap. But will you come? You are the man we need!"

John: Yes. I'll give it a go. I hope I don't regret it.

Archbishop: You won't, you won't. God will guide and bless you.

At the time the archbishop must have thought this a very good idea for it brought him a double benefit: his waste lands were brought back into cultivation and he would be able to recruit a better trained and (hopefully) a better brained man to work in his diocese than would otherwise have been possible. And, at first, it would not be bad news for Wetwang and Fridaythorpe. In the dark years after 1066 the archbishops must have had little time to ask 'What news from Wetwang ?' But now there was to be someone with the archbishop's ear and under the archbishop's eye with the responsibility of ensuring that Wetwang was again a viable and thriving community. But in the long run this gift of the archbishop probably did him no good and certainly did Wetwang great harm. For the archbishop's (imaginary) prophecy that one day the Wetwang prebend would be 'worth a good deal' proved to be true. It became one of the 'Golden Stalls' of York Minster, greatly sought after by those seeking a large income with a minimum of work. Some of archbishop Thomas's contemporaries criticized his generosity in giving away so much of his land to the cathedral and its prebends. For the gift was irrevocable and thereafter the only benefit the archbishop had was the right to appoint a new prebendary of Wetwang whenever the prebend fell vacant. And that was usually only when the previous prebendary had died. Nor could the archbishop charge a fee or sell the post to the highest bidder, as might be done with a new conveyance of a piece of land, for that would be illegal and the deadly sin of simony. So almost inevitably this rich gift was used to win the support of some great person – king, pope, or nobleman- to whom the archbishop owed a favour, or even to enrich his own family.

No doubt the archbishop felt he was ensuring the support of a powerful voice in Rome when he gave the Wetwang prebend to Cardinal Gaetano – who became pope in 1277, taking the name of Nicholas III. (Apparently one of the better popes who, a contemporary chronicler says 'would not have had his like upon the earth if only he had had no relatives to whom to show excessive favours'.) That same vice (nepotism) centuries later in 1582, ensured that archbishop Sandys made his son Edwin, a layman, prebendary of Wetwang and that he, before his death in 1602, so arranged the Wetwang leases that the income remained with his family till at least 1714.

And there is no doubt that, in the long run the creation of the prebend was bad news for Wetwang. We do not know how an adequate pastoral care was given to the people of these villages by a York-based prebendary in the early days of the prebend. But in 1240 the archbishop 'ordained vicarages' for Wetwang and Fridaythorpe. This meant that there was to be a full time resident priest in each village with a lifelong security of tenure. (i.e he couldn't be sacked). That was the good news. But these welcome appointments were to be financed by giving them only a tiny share of the tithes. This has meant that over the centuries most of the tithes that were originally meant to support a local ministry have gone to distant – often lay- owners with no interest at all in Wetwang or Fridaythorpe and no intention of spending locally any of the money they were exacting from the hard-working farming communities. And so little of the tithe income was left for the resident vicars that, once the idea of a married clergy was accepted, it no longer provided a living wage. So for centuries neither Fridaythorpe or Wetwang had a full-time resident vicar.

There were two further, perhaps surprising, results from archbishop Thomas's generosity. The first was that, ecclesiastically, Wetwang became 'a peculiar'. This meant that it was taken out of the jurisdiction of the archdeacon, rural dean, and the church courts of the rest of the diocese of York. These church courts, before modern times, played a significant part in people's ordinary lives. They had authority in everything to do with marriage and wills and were also concerned with the moral welfare of the parishioners from matters sexual (notably adultery and bastardy) down to neighbourly brawling. It is difficult to tell whether people were better off having these matters dealt with in 'The Peculiar Court of the Prebendary of Wetwang' than in the more usual Ecclesiastical Courts. It must often have been the same legal officers who officiated in each.

Then, secondly, that part of Wetwang that belonged to the prebendary became part of 'The Liberty of St Peter'. From the remotest past York Minster's claim to have its own civil courts and so to be exempt from the jurisdiction of the County magistrates seems to have been generally accepted. This 'Liberty of St Peter' was a county within the county. Then by a double fiction as the prebends of St Peter's York (i.e. York Minster) were canons of the cathedral their lands also were to be treated as belonging to York Minster and then, too, all these lands were to be thought of as actually contiguous to the Minster. In a place like Wetwang where part of the township was in the Liberty of St Peter and the rest in the East Riding it must have taken a good deal of pragmatic commonsense to ensure the smooth working of local government.

Astonishingly these oddities of both ecclesiastical and secular jurisdiction persisted into the nineteenth century. An Order of Council of 1846 and legislation of 1857 abolished all the ecclesiastical peculiars – except for some Royal peculiars such as Westminster Abbey and St George's Windsor. And, earlier, in 1837 the officials of the Liberty of St Peter quietly decided that it need no longer struggle to survive. Quaint and unusual though these anomalies were, I don't think anyone mourned their passing.

AN INTERLUDE : A RUSH THROUGH THE CENTURIES

The way we number the centuries can be confusing: of course we all know that in the twentieth century (from which we have just escaped) all the years from 1900 to 1999 began with 19. It is more difficult to remember, for example, that in the twelfth century each year begins with 11 -1120 or 1197- and that in the sixteenth century they all begin with 15 – Henry VIII came to the throne in 1509.

The Middle Ages can be a bit confusing too. But usually it means roughly the four centuries between the Norman conquest in 1066 and the Reformation from 1530 onwards. We can be helped to keep our bearings if we think of these centuries a bit like this:

Twelfth century (1100-1199) Good News. Growing prosperity and a steady growth of population.

Thirteenth century (1200-1299) Good News. Population continues to increase. New villages established out on the less fertile soils.

Fourteenth century (1300-1399) Very bad news. Changing climate (it got a good bit wetter and colder), over population and exhausted soils brought some famine conditions. The Scottish Wars led to desructive invasions. Above all, the Black Death from 1348 onwards killed up to half the population and persisted intermittently for the next three hundred years.

Fifteenth century (1400-1499) Getting better for the survivors. But continuing bad weather and The Wars of the Roses still make this a century you would be wise to miss when travelling in your Time Machine.

Sixteenth century (1500-1599) It all depends on your point of view: bad news – the end of the glorious 'age of faith' of Catholic England; good news – the beginning of the modern world with the shaking off of the shackles of superstition and the beginnings of parliamentary democracy.

4. THE TWELTH CENTURY: THE BUILDING OF THE CHURCHES

The Twelfth Century brought some boom years to Yorkshire. The new king, Henry I (1100-1135) brought in a new wave of Norman landowners,' men possibly less fastidious than William the Conqueror's followers and more willing to eat the oaten bread of these northern lands'. They soon turned into home-bred Yorkshiremen and invested their wealth in the great new monasteries – Kirkham, Rievaulx, Fountains, St Mary's York, and many, many others- in the first half of the 12th century. Then they built churches -they came up, it was said 'like mushrooms in the night'. The archbishop also prospered: In 1065 his lands had been worth annually £320. By 1086, thanks to William's brutal peace keeping, that had shrunk to £166. But less than a century later, in 1180 he was receiving £1180.

Wetwang and Fridaythorpe benefitted from the growing prosperity. By 1140 they each had a new stone church. It seems likely that, like most of the parishes with new 12th century stone churches, they already had wooden churches, possibly on the same site and just possibly very ancient indeed. Possibly too, the churchyards at both Wetwang and Fridaythorpe are older, and maybe much older, than the churches which stand in their midst. From the earliest times the careful burial of the dead and respect for places where the bones of the ancestors lay seems to have been something which united the successive generations, with their varying cultures and patterns of religious belief, that lived in and around these villages. And, for the most part, they buried their dead away from their homes and usually close to the frontiers of their communities. Yet in these planned and christian villages of the 11th (or earlier) centuries the burial ground is at the very heart of the village. At Wetwang the placing of the Church so far from what must always have been the village street is puzzling. Could it be because part of the churchyard was already well filled with bodies?

Our learned vicar, the Rev E Maule Cole gives archbishop Thurstan the credit for the building of Wetwang church. I can see him taking the prebendary of Wetwang on one side and telling him that it was high time he actually did something about those new churches needed at Wetwang and Fridaythorpe. He was not a man to be crossed! He was archbishop from 1119 to 1140 and a great man- 'the outstanding personality in Northern England.' He was a generous supporter of the new monasteries and played a major part in the founding of Fountains abbey and -archbishops were different in those days- led the clergy and nobility of the North against the Scottish invaders to the great victory of the battle of the Standard at Northallerton in 1138. It could be that some of the men of Wetwang and Fridaythorpe were directly involved in that battle. For we are told that the archbishop 'summoned the priest from every parish in the diocese, with cross, banners and relics going ahead and his arms-bearing parishioners marching behind'.

Many of our local churches can be dated to this period: a surviving inscription enables us to date Weaverthorpe fairly precisely to 1120; Kirkburn had become attached to Guisborough priory in 1119 and Garton to Kirkham priory in 1121 and it is probable that the churches were built soon after; Wharram-le-Street is, it seems the oldest of these churches taking us back to, say, 1090. The distinctive feature of all these churches is that, in an area with no decent building stone (chalk is rubbish) and with no ancient tradition of quarrying stone or building with it, they were all built with good quality, well cut stone much of which is still as it left the stonemason's hands over nine hundred years ago.

The new Wetwang church would have looked much like the churches we see today at Kirkburn or Wharram-le-Street – though it is likely that when it was finished the walls would be limewashed inside and out. It must have been a cause of wonder in a neighbourhood where nearly all the buildings were made of wood

The Church at Wharram-le-Street

and mud. Presumably the prebendary financed the enterprise and arranged to borrow some skilled stonemasons from York Minster. It had two 'rooms' with a nave 37ft long and a chancel of, very precisely, 17 feet and 4 inches. Although this first stone church was soon to be much extended and about a hundred years ago was very thoroughly 'restored', a good deal of the original building can still be seen – notably two of the windows on the south side of the nave (and much of that wall) some of the pillars and, of course, much of the original stone would be used in the extensions. (In the 1901 restoration many inscribed stones from that earliest church were uncovered and can now be seen both in the walls of the church and in the lych-gate.) Some sixty years later the nave was made 15½ feet longer (the join is very visible) and the tower built. Slightly oddly the tower is built a foot or so into the nave. An exactly similar arrangement can be seen in the ruined church in the deserted village of Wharram Percy. There the tower was never very stable and has now fallen down. It is surprising that Wetwang's tower has not gone the same way, for excavation has shown that its only foundation was numerous gravestones. It was a wise precaution to be content with a rather modest tower – though it became slightly less modest in the 15th century with the addition of the ornamental battlement round the top. Earlier, 1n 1260 according to G.E.Street, the great architect responsible for many of Sir Tatton Sykes new churches, the big north transept was built, which was one day to be a schoolroom and is now again the Lady Chapel. The arch on the south wall of the nave suggests that there was once a south transept as well but there are no traces of it. (Perhaps it was planned and then funds ran out and it was never built.)

Fridaythorpe was not blessed with an antiquarian vicar so there has to be even more guesswork than at Wetwang. The astonishingly ambitious south doorway ('utterly barbaric..with decorated scallops, zigzag -any old thing that was going' says Pevsner) takes us back to 1140 and this is the date of the main body of the church. The tower came fifty years later. Fridaythorpe was always a small and not very rich place. This means that the church has come to us more as it left those first builders' hands and chisels. It must have been growing population that led to the building of a north aisle in the 13th century and then a few centuries later, a shrinking population that permitted its demolition. The stone was used to block up the arches. (Perhaps misguidedly, it was rebuilt in 1901.)

Fridaythorpe church has an unsolved mystery: on the pillar nearest the chancel is carved the message 'This 713 found hear'. Churches were being built in 713 – but very rarely indeed in stone. Could this pillar have been here in

713? It would be nice to think so...but... Surprisingly there is an Anglo-Saxon peacock that has strayed to the west end of the rebuilt north aisle and, a good deal more visible, a mass-clock outside on the south wall. This is a sort of sundial said to help the priest to say mass at the right time. (Time-keeping must have been a problem in the clockless world of the Middle Ages, but I struggle to see how this would really help).

I've left the most important link between these two ancient churches and ourselves to the last. These are the fonts. Each is carved out of a single piece of jurassic rock. They go back to the very beginning of church life in these villages and could be older than the churches themselves – you can have a wooden church but you can't have a wooden font. These huge stone fonts were clearly very important to the Norman church builders in this neighbourhood. Sometimes they are elaborately carved as at Cowlam, Cottam (now in Langtoft), Bainton and Kirkburn, but even when, as here at Wetwang and Fridaythorpe, they are comparatively plain, they are noble and awe-inspiring works of art. For perhaps a thousand years nearly every child born in these villages has been christened in them. They deserve to be honoured and respected – and just occasionally hugged.

This great Twelfth century building programme in both village churches and monasteries involved, to use the modern jargon, a great financial investment in the local infra-structure. And, sticking for a moment with the jargon, they must have have used up a very significant proportion of the Gross National Product. The money was well spent. It seems unlikely that our own comparable investment in power-stations, motorways, or even hospitals and schools will still be in functional use nine hundred years hence! Their survival reflects both the fact that the job was well done in the beginning, but also the conscientious care with which they have been loved and used over the

The Font at Wetwang

centuries. We need to be grateful for an infinite number of acts of generosity - often unrecorded- through the centuries. To rebuild any one of these churches today, even with all the resources of our modern technology, would cost two or three million pounds. It is alarming, and just possibly absurd, that the care and responsibility for these churches today depends on the dedicated commitment of a tiny group of usually elderly and distinctly un-rich people.

Curiously, for both Wetwang and Fridaythorpe there has been recent uncertainty about the ancient dedication of their churches. Invariably an ancient church had a dedication nearly always to a saint. If at all possible there would be some relic of that saint (probably of very doubtful authenticity) incorporated in the altar. But after the 16th century the name of the saint could be forgotten as the custom grew of simply speaking of Fridaythorpe Church. The early authority in these matters, 'Lawton's Collections', (my copy was published in 1843) tells us that Wetwang is dedicated to St Michael but, unusually, gives no dedication for Fridaythorpe.

Before 1911 few ever doubted that we were St Michael's, Wetwang. In 1902 the Vicar, whose knowledge of matters mediaeval was unrivalled made sure that St Michael should be the dominant figure in the east window of the newly built chancel. Yet the chalice and paten still used at every Communion Service are almost aggressively inscribed 'St Nicholas Church, Wetwang 1911'.

For after a reign of 46 years the old vicar had died and in 1911 Wetwang had a new vicar. He must have read, or listened to, Canon Raine, another learned York cleric who argued that our true patron saint was St Nicholas. I have yet to track down where Canon Raine says this but I presume it is because of the latin inscription on our mediaeval bell 'St Nicholas pray for us'. But we do not know why Canon Raine failed to convince the learned Mr Cole or why the new vicar decided to begin his ministry so dramatically with a change of name for the church. It has taken a long time for the new name to take firm root. Up to 1991 Crockford's Clerical Directory continued to say that 'though Wetwang was anciently dedicated to St Nicholas it is now called St Michael' and on many maps the name 'St Michael' survives.

Fridaythorpe is simpler. In 1982 it belongs to St James. In 1992 it has become St Mary. Who made the change? and why? Today in an admirable spirit of compromise the church is dedicated to St James and St Mary. But it is unlikely that 'St James' was the original dedication. He wasn't that popular in 1140.

5. THE DOUBLE MYSTERY OF FIMBER

The Second Mystery needs to be dealt with first. This only came to light when preparations were being made for the building of the new church. This replaced an ancient chapel-of-ease which is picturesquely described in Mr Edmonson's 1857 History of Fimber: 'This small ancient building stands on an eminence situate in the midst of a fruitful garden. There is the evergreen and the woodbine twining themselves over the roof of the little edifice. There is also the dwarf apple tree, the gooseberry tree...all growing luxuriantly and catching the eye of the traveller as he passes by'. This 'ancient edifice' may have been destroyed by fire, as some say, but was certainly pulled down in 1868 to make way for the new church on the same site. Which bring us to the mystery. Whilst excavating for the foundations of the 1871 church the foundations were found of a church much larger and apparently more ancient than the 'little edifice' that had just been demolished. Fimber had always been thought of as a small chapel-of-ease to Wetwang. But once, it would seem, there had stood here a church as grand and as ancient as Wetwang itself. Only rarely is serious excavation possible beneath an ancient church. This excavation, conducted by J.R.Mortimer himself, showed that the mound on which the church had been built was an artificial creation. (The two Fimber ponds might have been the result of the digging needed to raise this mini-mountain) Apparently this mound was an oval barrow containing a crouched Beaker burial and an Anglo-Saxon burial with buckle, about 80 yards from a cemetery of furnished Anglo-Saxon graves. The situation is very similar to Goodmanham. There, according to the Venerable Bede was a pagan Anglo-Saxon 'temple'. More recently scholars have suggested that there might have been another such 'temple' at Fimber. If so, the memory of it, (as at Goodmanham), might have been a reason for building a church on this 'holy hill'. But if such a church had been built in Anglo-Saxon times it would have been of wood, and any traces of it are unlikely to have survived. We need another explanation.

The first, and more ancient, of the Fimber Mysteries may well give an answer to the second. This is, simply, why is Fimber not in the Domesday Book? Tiny places like Raisthorpe, Burdale, and Towthorpe get a mention so why is Fimber overlooked? Rather curiously the unravelling of this Domesday mystery begins with the De Tosny family and the part they played in the foundation of St Mary's Abbey at York.

Robert de Tosny came from Normandy with the Conqueror and was rewarded with lands in thirteen counties including Yorkshire. By the time of the Domesday Book in 1086 most of his Yorkshire lands had been handed on to his second son, Berengar de Tosny. And though he still held his lands at North Dalton and Naburn, the record notes that 'Berengar his son holds of him'. The list of Berengar's Yorkshire lands is a long one and in the East Riding includes Duggleby, Settrington, Burythorpe and Heathfield (Higrefelt).

St Mary's Abbey at York was going to become the richest Benedictine monastery in the North of England. But the story of the foundation in 1086 is far from straightforward. We need to go back to William the Conqueror's 'Harrying of the North' in 1069. Reinfrid was a knight who was with William on that campaign. He happened to visit Whitby and was distressed at the scene of desolation at that once-famous abbey. (He had read his Venerable Bede.) Resolving to become a monk he joined the community at Evesham – for none of the northern monasteries had survived the 9th century Danish invasions. In 1073, with two companions he returned to the north and, having searched out the ruins of the ancient monasteries, settled at Jarrow. But Reinfrid had not forgotten Whitby. William de Percy was another Norman knight who linked his fortunes to those of the Conqueror. Whitby had become one of those Yorkshire possessions which were to be the foundation of the fortunes of the greatest (and longest lasting) of north country families. In 1078 Reinfrid persuaded William to refound Whitby abbey. But the distinctly villainous William's involvement in the abbey proved hazardous. Not only did 'he regret his generosity' and try to get the lands he had given back, but also insisted that members of his family should remain in control. His son, another William, became the first abbot. This led to some dissension and a group of monks left to found a new monastery at nearby Lastingham, 'the last resting place of St Chad'. In a complex tale the new king, William Rufus, became involved and the Lastingham monks were persuaded to commit themselves to a much more ambitious venture – the building of a vast new monastery as a rival to the ancient minster and cathedral at York. This had the enthusiastic support of the new Norman land-owning class – except for archbishop Thomas who saw this as a serious threat to his plans for his cathedral and its prebendaries. He must have suspected that there was a hidden agenda of making the monastery the cathedral as at Durham and Canterbury. But the abbey was built -the extensive remains can still be seen almost next door to the minster- and the cathedral survived unscathed. (What on earth has all this to do with Fimber you must be asking? Be patient: we are nearly there.)

The de Tosny family were amongst the earliest supporters of the new monastery. As early as Domesday Book (1086) Berengar had given land at Lastingham to 'the abbot' and at Kirby Misperton to 'the abbot of York'. This suggests that he actively supported both the move from Whitby to Lastingham and also the further move to York. Fimber's name (Finmere actually) is first preserved in writing in the earliest surving cartulary (list of possessions) of St Mary's Abbey, York. This is dated 1121 and tells us that Berengar de Tosny gave the abbey 9½ carucates (about 1000 acres) at Finmere. There can be no doubt that this was one of the foundation gifts of the new abbey and thus can be dated as soon after 1086. In 1085 Berengar would have given a detailed account of all his lands to the Domesday Commissioners. It would make no sense for him to conceal his 9½ carucates at Finmere. Therefore they must be in Domesday Book somewhere. There are two possibilities. The first is the 'sokeland' -6 carucates and 6 bovates- attached to North Dalton. The second is the much smaller 'Higrefelt'. This gets translated as 'Heathfield' but I can find no 'Heathfield' anywhere in the area. I'm pretty certain that one, or perhaps both, of these entries should be marked 'aka Fimber'.

(There is another possibility. Perhaps Berengar had given his Fimber lands to the abbot before the Domesday inquiries were made and thought it was for him to put them into the return. But it seems that the abbot was able to slip through the Domesday net. He comes fourth in the list of landowners with which the Yorkshire Domesday begins – after the king, the archbishop and the bishop of Durham. But in the body of the book he has no entry at all.)

This not quite the end of the story. At much the same time William Rufus gave Elmswell (and three other 'berewicks' around Driffield) to St Mary's abbey. It seems that, despite its long past history, Elmswell at that time was uncultivated and uninhabited and that it was only after the gift to the abbey that the village was reoccupied and brought back into cultivation. It seems likely that the same was true of Fimber. Then, conscientiously the monks began to have built a church for their new village and, perhaps with some idea that this was a 'holy hill', resolved to make it bigger and better than the average village church. Then -this of course is pure speculation- they found themselves faced with the fury of an already very angry archbishop: 'How dare you build a church in **my** parish of Wetwang?' The monks caved in (or did a deal): 'Yes,yes, we've now seen your maps and recognize that Fimber is well within your parish of Wetwang. But the land did belong to Berengar and it now belongs to us. But we will leave the building of the church to your man and trust that he will see to the proper pastoral care of our people there.' And so it came about that Fimber, though it had never belonged to the archbishop, was undoubtedly in the parish of Wetwang and the spiritual responsibility of the rector, the prebendary of Wetwang. But until the dissolution in 1539 most of the land belonged to St Mary's abbey at York. That something like that imaginary confrontation did take place is confirmed by the unusual special mention given to Fimber a hundred years later when the arrangements are made to ensure that there are resident vicars at both Fridaythorpe and Wetwang. The vicar of Wetwang is to be paid a little extra because of his additional responsibilities at Fimber. Though, until very recently, Fimber was never, strictly speaking, a parish church, its early history made it rather more than a chapel-of-ease. The Revd E M Cole probably got it right when he called his parish 'Wetwang-cum-Fimber'.

A NOTE ON TOWTHORPE

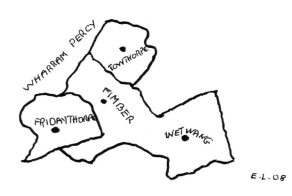

Strictly speaking Towthorpe is trespassing here. For undoubtedly it was part of the unfortunate parish of Wharram Percy. ('Unfortunate' because though the parish was probably founded about 1150 to serve the five villages of Wharram Percy, Thixendale, Raisthorpe, Burdale and Towthorpe, only Thixendale survived into modern times as an inhabited village.) Thixendale became a separate parish in 1870 and presumably it was sometime after that that Towthorpe drifted into the Fimber-Wetwang parish.

(Fimber and Towthorpe became a joint civil parish in, I think, 1935) But as it is now certainly part of the 2½ parishes of this book's title it has earned a mention.

Towthorpe has three entries in Domesday Book. In the 'summary' we learn that the king had 6 carucates and his half-brother, the count of Mortain, had three. It must be doubtful that either really knew that they had the privilege of owning part of Towthorpe. More interestingly, Domesday also tells us that Orm lives on the count's land and that Lagman and Sunulf have two ploughs on the king's land and that it is worth 30 shillings. These men, with Arnbiorn at Fridaythorpe, are the first of our fellow parishioners we know by name. Towthorpe is Tove's Thorp. The name is common among the Danes and, indeed, all these names have a danish ring to them. Towthorpe, like Wetwang, was a planned village. That by the 17th century it had become depopulated except for the one farm at the centre (later to be divided into two) has made it possible to reconstruct the ancient layout of the land with the help of old maps, aerial photography and a ground survey. The land is laid out regularly in strips running north to south – sometimes more than 1,000 yards long. The foundations of the deserted houses can be clearly seen. And from 1325 there was a chapel in the village, dedicated to St Catherine, which was to fall victim to royal rapacity in 1548. And as a village Towthorpe was passing into history. This happened because one family there, the Taylors, gradually bought out everybody else. There were still eleven houses in 1672. But when the last Taylor died in 1724 he was able to bequeath the whole of Towthorpe to his son-in-law John Graeme. A hundred years later another John Graeme divided the land into two farms. The Megginsons came to Towthorpe in 1762, rented one of the farms in 1824 and have been there ever since. By 2001 they had reunited the two farms and become the contented owners of almost all of Towthorpe.

POSTSCRIPT: VILLAGE CHRISTIANITY BEFORE 1066

As we have seen, nearly all our local parish churches were built in the early 12th century. But we know that by the early 8th century the Anglo-Saxon peoples had been, at least nominally, converted to Christianity. And though the Danish invasions and settlement in the next century led to a great deal of destruction of monasteries and disruption of diocesan organisation, before long the newcomers seems to have accepted the religion of their Anglo-Saxon neighbours. But how were people given pastoral care, opportunities for worship, and having their babies christened and their dead buried in these centuries? We do not really know. But it does seem that the usual pattern was not that of a church and a priest in every village. Instead each neighbourhood was focussed on a central, well resourced, church centre staffed by a number of clergy. These centres were called 'minsters' and in later ages when ordinary parish churches had come to abound, 'old minsters'. The Latin for 'minster' is 'monasterium' and that can also be translated as 'monastery'. But though some minsters might have been monasteries many were not. The name is familiar to us from York minster and Beverley minster and at Beverley minster the ancient limits of the minster parish give us some idea of how these big 'Minster Parishes' worked. There is some evidence that Pickering, Pocklington, Old Malton, Kilham, Hunmanby, Bridlington and Driffield may all have been 'Old Minsters'. Was York minster a minster as well as a cathedral? Was there an area around it to which the clergy gave pastoral care? And were we part of it? If we were it would give some justification for the development of the prebends. But if we were, how did these distant clergy minister to us? We do not know. But we do know that, long before the days of building village churches, it was the custom to put up large crosses both to remind people of the fundamental truths of their Christian faith and to mark the spot where the community could meet with the itinerant priest from the -perhaps distant- minster. In Wetwang churchyard there may be the base of just such a cross. It seems to have had a curiously peripatetic journey from Holmfield to Wetwang Main Street and then to the churchyard. But it is at least possible that this rather undistinguished-looking stone is a tangible point of contact with the ancient beginnings of Christianity in the Wolds. Our churchyards themselves might be another such link. The clearest mark of distinction been the christian and the pre-christian community was in their choice of burial ground. In earlier ages the dead had been buried at the outer limits of the cultivated fields, whilst for the christians the dead were to be buried at the heart of the village. It may well be that our churchyards are centuries older than the church building itself. Perhaps our parish churches are really cemetery chapels!

6. CENTURIES WITHOUT CHANGE? 1150 – 1500

For us today, the changes that a decade can bring -mobile phones and the internet? – can be mind boggling. And for those of us who can look back to a pre-1945 childhood it does really seem to others as though we came from another planet. This can make it difficult for us to grasp that for generation after generation the lifestyles of those who lived here before us hardly changed at all. The poet Thomas Hardy gets it about right (though it should have been 'ox' not 'horse'):

> "Only a man harrowing clods
> In a slow silent walk
> With an old horse that stumbles and nods
> Half asleep as they stalk.
> Only a thin smoke without flame
> From the heaps of couch grass;
> Yet this will go onward the same
> Though Dynasties pass."

So before we leave the Middle Ages and let this 'Wetwang Saga' sweep us into the turmoil of the 16th century it is worth looking back over the previous four centuries to – say 1150 – and check on the things that never changed... and those that did.

CHURCHES AND MONASTERIES

All the churches that were here in 1500 (and indeed in 1800) had been built by 1150. And as this was an area of only modest prosperity they were largely spared ambitious rebuilding projects – an extra aisle here or there was about the best they could do. The churches we see today at Wetwang, Fridaythorpe, Garton, Kirkburn, Wharram-le-Street and many another, even with Victorian restorations, would be easily recognizable by a visitor from the late 12th century. (Bainton is the exception – it was entirely rebuilt in about 1335)

The 12th century too, with one exception, saw the building of the monasteries, great and small, that were to dominate the neighbourhood for the next four hundred years: Bridlington in 1113, Kirkham in 1122, Warter in 1132, and Watton, Malton and Nunburnholme (and many others) around 1150. Haltemprice (near Cottingham), not founded till 1326, is the odd man out. That the monasteries, like the cathedrals, were ambitiously rebuilt in the centuries that followed their foundation shows who had gained most from the 12th century redistribution of the resources of the church.

Each of these village Parish Churches would have its own resident parish priest. The names of these vicars and the dates of their institution to the living have survived in episcopal records since about 1300. The names suggest that they were very often local lads much of whose limited training and education would have been received from their local vicar. Surprisingly, despite the smallness of most of these parishes, there seems to have been an abundance of assistants. Some would be priests and in some parishes there would be an endowment of some sort for a chantry priest. Others would be semi-laymen in minor orders – acolytes and doorkeepers perhaps. When a living fell vacant the archbishop would see it was quickly filled from this pool of under-employed and underpaid clergy. The institution of the new incumbent would follow within four or five weeks of the death of his predecessor. Though the compulsory celibacy of the clergy had become the rule of the church it is unlikely that it was strictly observed in rural Yorkshire. Many of the earliest names on the list of vicars have a local village name as the surname. The first named vicar of Wetwang is 'Richard, son of Austin of Wetwang'. Was he the son of a previous vicar? These rural clergy were literally 'working class' – for not only were they by birth part of the local community but they would also share in the work of the fields in which they had their own allotted strips.

The services in the parish church would be almost unchanged from the time of the building of the church in the 12th century till the changes brought in by the Tudor monarchs in the 16th century. The mass, in latin, would be said or sung – possibly every day. Certainly on Sunday everybody would be there. Inevitably, as the church was the only public building in the village it would be used for a wide variety of public activities. Was it heated? Probably not.

The monasteries too had their unchanging routines for nearly four hundred years. After the excitements of the founding generation numbers quickly stabilised at a level that was fairly strictly related to the financial resources of the monastery. Roughly speaking the numbers of monks and nuns in each house was much the same in 1500 as it had been in 1200. Of those near to us the nuns at Nunburnholme were the poorest in Yorkshire with only a handful of sisters- yet they maintained the life of their nunnery without interruption, and with hardly any public history for nearly four hundred years. The Augustinian canons at Warter were a good deal more prosperous and the canons and nuns at Watton -it was a double monastery – were positively rich. Richest of all was St Mary's at York and its over-wealthy abbot figures regularly in the Robin Hood legends. It is difficult to tell what sort of relationships there were between the local churches and the monasteries -great and small- in their neighbourhood. The Kirkham canons may have had some sort of branch house at Sledmere. The fine churches at Garton and Kirkburn were almost certainly built through the generosity of the priories of Kirkham and Guisborough. But though the monasteries hardly changed at all in these centuries in numbers or lifestyle the canons of Kirkham, for example, must often have felt they were living on a building site. Visiting there today we can study the remains of the 12th century nave, the 13th century choir, and the domestic buildings of the 14th and 15th centuries. Remembering that Kirkham was not a big player in the monastic world, we can only marvel at the scale of the enterprise and not be surprised to hear that the rebuilding of the choir nearly bankrupted the priory.

In land ownership, after the upheavals of the Norman takeover hardly anything changed for four hundred years. This was largely because of the 'dead hand' of the church. From 1200 onwards a series of 'Statutes of Mortmain' struggled to prevent further gifts of land to the church. It is linguistically odd that the 'hand'(main) of the church is 'dead'(mort)

Kirkham Priory

simply because the church never dies. Though bishops, abbots and vicars were as mortal as the rest of us, the institution they served lived on. The whole of Wetwang, very nearly all of Fimber, and much of Fridaythorpe belonged to the church in one way or another. This meant that very nearly everybody had the same landlord in 1500 as they had had in 1200.

The use made of the land too can hardly have changed either. Economically England remained overwhelmingly an agricultural community. An open field village had to be a co-operative community with very little scope for individual enterprise. The lack of artificial fertilisers meant that the productivity of the land was limited to what could be achieved by fallowing and the careful use of the limited animal manure. The weather was all important and the worsening climate after the 12th century increased the dangers of famine. A slow change was the gradual replacement of the ox by the horse as the farm's working animal – but this was not complete till the end of the 18th century. (And I'm told that even today an ox or two can be found ploughing away in some odd corner of England).

But, of course, great events did dramatically disturb the even course of these 'centuries without change' and, inevitably, these must sometimes have impacted a great deal on Fimber, Fridaythorpe and Wetwang.

The Scottish Wars really began in earnest with the attempt of the first king Edward, after the death of the direct heir to the Scottish throne in 1290, to bring Scotland under his control. This made the north of England a centre of royal concern with Parliaments meeting in York and even the king staying in the archbishop's manor at Wetwang. But a royal visitor was an expensive privilege. The ancient law of 'purveyance' placed the responsibility for feeding the King and those travelling with him on the local community. Much more serious than the cost of entertaining the king was the fact that the long term failure of his plans resulted in a series of Scottish invasions. Northumberland suffered most but there were times when the invaders spread their destruction far down into Yorkshire. The rebuilding of Bainton Church in 1335 was a consequence of the destruction of the earlier building by a Scottish army.

But more serious than the dangers of war were the perils of disease. Almost certainly the most terrible event in Wetwang's long history was the coming of the **Black Death.** Though there are records of outbreaks of what seems to be bubonic plague intermittently throughout ancient times, the outbreak, known to later history as 'the Black Death', seems to have begun in Southern Russia in 1346. There the Genoans, defending their small Crimean trading post against a vast army of Moslem Tartars were astonished when 'the pride of the infidel invaders was humbled as they rapidly died with marks on their bodies and lumps in their joints. Whereupon the Tartars, worn out by this pestilential disease... ordered the corpses to be placed upon their engines and thrown into the city so that the Christians were not able to protect themselves from this danger'. The terrible stratagem worked. The plague spread amongst the Genoans. The survivors fled to their ships and -fatally- sailed back home to Genoa. The plague spread rapidly through Europe and reached England in May or June 1348. 'The Great Mortality' (which was the usual name given by contemporaries) seems to have reached Hull by the end of that year. It then spread quickly along the Humber and its tributaries in the early spring of 1349. The first deaths in York were on Ascension Day 1349. June, July and August were the worst months all over the north of England. We cannot exaggerate the horror of the Black Death. There was no known cure and ignorance until recently of the sources of infection- the black house rat and the fleas it carried – meant that the only remotely effective defence was flight from the infected areas. The archbishop of York believed that 'the great pestilence, mortality and infection of the air...must be caused by the sins of men' and that the remedy must be 'repentance with prayer, processions and litanies'.

Recent careful research gives support to the grim accounts of the contemporary chroniclers. In Meaux Abbey (near Hull) the abbot and five monks died on one day and only ten of the fifty monks survived. It is becoming accepted that nearly half of the population really did die from the Black Death. And in the years after 1349 there were repeated, though with decreasing frequency, outbreaks of the plague until the last great outbreak in London (and Eyam near Sheffield) in 1666. Slightly worryingly, as the experts don't really know why the plague went away from England, they cannot guarantee that it will never return.

And were Fridaythorpe and Wetwang spared? Almost certainly not. We have no precise historical data from those days for if there were burial registers none have survived. But the archbishop's registers of the institution of new vicars still survive. Almost invariably, unless the register records otherwise, the arrival of a new vicar meant that his predecessor had died within the previous six weeks. Appallingly we discover that Wetwang, Fridaythorpe, Wharram Percy, Wharram-le-Street, Kirby Grindalythe, Kirby Underdale, and Settrington all had a vicar dying in 1349. Bugthorpe and Sherburn both had two institutions in that fatal year. That William of Grimston survived as rector of Cowlam from 1320 until 1364 may well be because he had the archbishop's licence to be absent from his parish. But there can be no real doubt that these villages lay at the heart of a severe outbreak of the plague with the inevitable consequence of a very heavy death rate.

Yet there would be some to gather in the harvest and prepare for the coming year. Philip Ziegler, who in 1963 wrote a marvellous account of the Black Death, notes that 'one of the most striking features of the Black Death in England...is the way in which communal life survived. With his friends and relations dying in droves around him, with labour lacking to till the fields and care for the cattle, with every kind of human intercourse rendered perilous by the possibility of infection, the mediaeval Englishman obstinately carried on in his wonted way. Business was very far from being as usual but landlord and peasant alike did their best to make it so.'

THE POLL TAXES AND THE PEASANTS REVOLT 1381

Inevitably a calamity like the Black Death had far reaching economic consequences. There were fewer mouths to feed and fewer hands to do the work. This meant that prices fell and wages rose. This was bad news for the landowners who found themselves struggling both to keep their land in cultivation and, even when it was being farmed by others, to make a profit out of it. And bad news for the Government who were faced with a continuing and expensive war with France whilst the yield from the traditional sources of revenue steadily dwindled. They responded with the Statute of Labourers of 1351 which tried to control wages and hinder the labourer's mobility. And the more traditionally minded landowners -notably the churchmen- made strenuous efforts to enforce their ancient rights to compulsory labour from those living on their land.

Then, in 1377 came the first Poll Tax. This demanded a groat (4d) from everyone except licensed beggars. It was meant to be a one-off payment to meet an exceptional financial crisis. It raised £22,000 and caused little upheaval. The temptation to repeat the experiment was irresistible. The 1380 Poll Tax was more complex with a graduated scale ranging from the £6.13s.4d charged to archbishops and dukes to the 4d expected from 'Simple Men and Women and poor Monks and Nuns'. To their surprise (for they had not yet learnt how adept the rich are at tax evasion) this raised much less than the first Poll Tax. So in 1381, with the third Poll Tax Parliament both reverted to the flat rate tax for everyone and tripled it to 12d. Many were unwilling, or unable, to pay and stern judicial commissions were sent out to enforce payment.

This was too much and resulted in the Peasants Revolt. This began in Kent and Essex and the rebels soon gained control of London. Their hatred was focussed on those who had imposed the Poll Tax, on those lawyers who struggled to enforce the Statute of Labourers and on those landlords who were insisting on their ancient rights. The archbishop of Canterbury was beheaded on Tower Green and many judges murdered. The young King Richard II survived by agreeing to the rebels' demands and then, of course, after the death of Wat Tyler, the leader of the revolt, by cancelling on July 4th the charters he had granted on June 14th.

All this was in and around London and East Anglia. Did it directly affect Wetwang? There were disturbances in Scarborough, York and Beverley. Did they spread to the villages? Was the 'Can't pay, Won't pay' chant of the modern Poll Tax rioters heard in Wetwang? We don't know. But we do know that 'twelve jurors from the Wapentake of Buckrose' (which includes all our villages) were amongst those called upon to investigate and adjudicate upon the the troubles in Scarborough.

We can sometimes be grateful that treasury bureaucrats are great hoarders of documents. Many of these village Poll Tax Rolls have survived and from them we can learn the actual names of those who were living here around 1380.

ARCHBISHOP SCROPE AND THE WARS OF THE ROSES

The teenage King, Richard II, showed great personal courage at the time of the Peasants' Revolt and was given much of the credit for the government's victory. His uncle, John of Gaunt, duke of Lancaster who had been running the country (very unsuccessfully) during king Richard's minority, and had become the most hated man in England, only survived the revolt by the chance that he was away in Scotland at the crucial time. But his son Henry was with the young king and would certainly have been beheaded with the archbishop of Canterbury if his escape from the Tower had failed. Nearly twenty years later the same Henry, now himself duke of Lancaster was to seize the throne from Richard II and at least acquiesce in his murder. This was the beginning of a century of civil war in which the families of Lancaster and York fought for the throne. In this struggle three kings, Henry VI, Edward V and Richard III were killed and the leading claimants to the throne beheaded or killed in battle. Peace did not return till in 1485 Henry Tudor, an illegitimate descendant of John of Gaunt (and so of the House of Lancaster) killed the Yorkist Richard

III and, then, by marrying Elizabeth of York, the late King's sister brought dynastic peace to England. The great heraldic symbol of the Tudor dynasty was the doubled white and red rose.

Did these dramatic, and at times horrific, events trouble Wetwang? Probably not. The Wars of the Roses apparently caused a minimum of economic disruption, hardly any destruction of property, and hardly any killing away from the battlefield. Yet Richard of York, whose claim to have a better right to the throne than Henry VI escalated the dispute into war, was seen very much as a Yorkshireman and there is evidence that public opinion in the north was very much on the Yorkist side. This explains why Henry VI's ferocious Queen, having defeated Richard, Duke of York at the battle of Wakefield demanded

'Off with his head, and set it on York gates

So York may overlook the town of York'.

But Wetwang could well have been more directly involved in the revolt of archbishop Scrope a generation earlier. Unusually amongst archbishops of York, he was a Yorkshireman, the son of Lord Scrope of Masham, one of the great Yorkshire magnates of the time. But it was his friendship with Richard II that made him archbishop of York in 1398. But when in the following year Henry of Lancaster,(landing at Ravenspur on the Humber), with the support of the Percy earl of Northumberland (then more of Leconfield than Alnwick) successfully claimed the throne, Scrope surprisingly supported the regime change and took part in his coronation as Henry IV. But he, and his Percy neighbours, quickly changed their minds and plotted a northern revolt against the usurper. "The people of York fervently supported their archbishop and were supported by 'gentle simple priests and villeins' who flocked into the city from his neighbouring countryside". But the archbishop, marching with his 'priestly rout' of 8000 men to join with the earl of Northumberland was tricked into negotiation, taken prisoner, and quickly beheaded in York before the archbishop of Canterbury could come to his rescue. He was the only archbishop of York (so far!) to die a violent death and despite the hostility of the Lancastrian kings, his tomb in York minster soon became a place of pilgrimage. Were priests and people from our parishes part of that disastrously led army? Very probably yes. Did they come to much harm? Probably not. The archbishop was taken prisoner at 'Slipton' says the old account. He was on his way to meet with Northumberland at Topcliffe. There is no 'Slipton' on my maps. But there is 'Shipton' only a few miles north of York on the direct route to Topcliffe. It must have been here that the army was 'disbanded' and hopefully the Wetwangers and their priest were able to make a weary, but peaceful, journey home.

Were these then 'Centuries without change'? Compared either with modern times or even the century that was to follow, we have to grant them an extraordinary degree of stability. Even the value of money was much the same in 1500 as 1200. Yet for those living here in 1500 three changes – none of which can be precisely dated – had made a great difference:

1. They now knew -rulers and ruled alike – that they were all English and everybody, except for some French with the lawyers and a lot of Latin in church, spoke and thought in English. We had become English nationalists.

2. They were all free. Rather mysteriously, for this cannot be dated by legislation (Richard II's charters of enfranchisement had been instantly annulled) those working on the land, though they may still be holding that land by the ancient copyholds of the manor were no longer tied to the land and no longer forced to do compulsory work for the landlord.

3. They knew about money. In 1200 they would hardly ever see money – for there were no copper coins for small change. But by 1500 you could go shopping; there might be a coin in your pocket for the alehouse and if you had the misfortune to be a landless labourer almost your whole living would be the small coin you were given at the end of the day.

Living in 1500 then, did you think you were living at the end of an age, that big changes were bound to come soon ? Certainly not! Many of our past troubles were over. There was only one king in England and no more threat of civil war. The long schism in the papacy was over and the pope sits securely on his throne in Rome. The weather was getting better and even the plague was less threatening. Driffield in 1500 was still just a village: the magnificent tower of the parish church (best seen from the Viking Centre car park) is a record of the confidence and prosperity of the generation of 1500.

The Church Tower at Wetwang

And here in Wetwang we took the brave decision to add an ornamental parapet to our rather squat tower – the first real addition to the church since the building of the Lady Chapel around 1260. They were ready for another three centuries without change.

7. HENRY VIII AND THE BEGINNINGS OF CHANGE

THE CALM BEFORE THE STORM

The peaceful accession of the eighteen year old Henry VIII to his father's throne in 1509 (the first such peaceful and undisputed accession for nearly a century) must have convinced most people that the era of civil turmoil was over and that this was to be a time of stability and prosperity. No one foresaw that this king was going to inaugurate the greatest national upheavals since the time of William the Conqueror.

Even twenty years later I doubt if even a breath of the coming winds of change had reached Wetwang. Martin Luther had started the Protestant Reformation with the nailing of his 95 theses to the church door at Wittenberg on All Saint's Eve (31st October) 1517 and the king himself (with the help of a ghostwriter?) had gained the gratitude of the pope, and the title of 'Defender of the Faith' by writing a refutation of these Lutheran heresies. But I doubt if news of any of this got much nearer to Wetwang than some gossip amongst the Baltic merchants of Hull. And though the clergy were less popular that they had once been and there was some grumbling at the wealth of the church the deep seated catholicism of the people of Wetwang (and the rest of England) remained unchallenged. It seems unlikely that any of our local clergy were highly educated but they would have enough latin to understand the liturgy that would be the daily nourishment of their parishioners and enough pastoral sensitivity to guide their people through the crises of birth, marriage, sickness and death. They would be expected to preach rarely if at all. But this somewhat negative report on the ministry of the mediaeval parish priest ignores two great truths: firstly that the liturgy itself, even though it was largely in an unknown language, by its familiarity and the drama of its presentation, made real to the people the great fact of their salvation through the birth, death, resurrection, and coming in glory and judgement of Jesus

Christ and secondly, that the Saints and the Angels were their living, active and powerful friends. It meant something that every time their church bell rang it carried to heaven the message 'St Nicholas, pray for us'. And it probably mattered a great deal that as near as Bridlington lay the shrine of the gentle prior, St John of Bridlington, (born and bred at Thwing) and at Beverley, that of St John of Beverley (born at Harpham) who, as everbody knew had, with his brother at Bridlington brought victory to the English army at Agincourt.

But hardly anyone was looking for, or remotely prepared for, change.

The unravelling of the old regime began gently. The King's desire for a new wife and a male heir could have passed with merely a passing whiff of scandal if it had not been for the involvement of the pope. Henry's wife, Catherine of Aragon had been previously married to Henry's older brother Arthur. After Arthur's death instead of returning to Spain she had married his brother. This marriage was only possible with a papal dispensation. If it could be argued that a pope had no such authority then the dispensation was invalid and Henry was not legally married to Catherine and so was free to marry Anne Boleyn. The news of all this would reach Wetwang with the consequent changes to the liturgy- 'Anne our Queen' instead of 'Catherine' and the removal of the name of the pope.

My guess is that people minded a little about Catherine -but 'is it really any of our business?' and not-at-all about the pope.

But if the pope 'had no authority in this realm of England' who was head of the church? The 1534 'Act of Supremacy' gives an unequivocal answer: 'The King's Majesty hath the chief power in this realm, unto whom the chief government of all Estates of this realm, whether they be Ecclesiastical or Civil, in all causes doth appertain, and is not, nor ought to be subject to any foreign Jurisdiction'. This claim to be 'head of the church' which was shocking, and even blasphemous, to some in 1534 (and probably incomprehensible to most people in 2008) was not simply an outbreak of a tyrant's megalomania but an intelligent, and intelligible, response to a problem that had beset christian Europe for many centuries. Everybody agreed that all power came from God. But to whom had God given the right to exercise that power in His name? Those first christian emperors (Constantine, with his York links, reigned in the early 4th century) never doubted that they were supreme and answerable to God alone. In the Middle Ages emperors and popes struggled for supremacy. The theory of the 'Two Swords' (St Luke 22.38) gave scope for compromise: the emperor was to run the state and the pope the church.

But later mediaeval popes would have none of this: the pope as successor to St Peter, was God's vicegerent on earth, and it was he who delegated the practical business of running a country to such secular rulers as he thought worthy. Though these grandiose claims were difficult to maintain in reality, they were never formally renounced. It was by an exercise of this power that in 1570 pope Paul V (subsequently canonized) deposed Elizabeth from the throne of England and urged the faithful to make this deposition a reality by her assassination. Henry's assertion of the Royal Supremacy was linked to his claim that 'England was an Empire' and so in no way answerable to the Holy Roman Emperor in Germany who claimed some rather vague oversight over mere kings as the successor of the old Roman emperors. As far as England was concerned, Henry, and only Henry (and his heirs and successors) held the powers that had once belonged to the Emperor Constantine. Since the time of Henry VIII all English rulers (except his daughter Mary) have maintained this Royal Supremacy and it was the fear of those papal claims that led Parliament, after their unfortunate experiences with the catholic convert James II, to make it law that the sovereign must neither be a Roman Catholic nor married to a Roman Catholic.

THE DISSOLUTION OF THE MONASTERIES

The Royal Supremacy, with its removal of the bishop of Rome from any role in the life of the English church, was to a small number of people literally a matter of life and death. They saw the attack on papal authority as an overthrow of the very fundamentals of the christian faith. Sir Thomas More, John Fisher, bishop of Rochester, and the monks of the London Charterhouse paid with their lives for their refusal to accept the change. But if this, perhaps linked to some necessary but modest reforms in the life of the church, had been the limit of Henry's policy, Wetwang, Fimber and Fridaythorpe might have dozed gently for another century or so. But, for better or worse, Henry (or at least his advisers) had two other aims: economic change and doctrinal reform. The king was keen for economic change. He needed more money if he was to make a mark in Europe comparable to that of the kings of France and Spain. From Cardinal Wolsey he had learnt that it was possible to close down some monasteries and divert their resources to a better use without too much outcry. In 1524, with the help of a Papal Bull, Wolsey had founded and funded Cardinal College, Oxford (now Christchurch) by the suppression of 21 monasteries and, rather oddly, the theft of the prebend of Wetwang.

Thomas Cromwell, having become Henry's chief minister, must have hinted to his master that there were easy pickings to be made at the expense of these, probably less loved and respected than they had once been, ancient foundations. As the King's Vicar-General he was able to absorb the disciplinary powers that normally belonged to the bishops and send inspectors (with the traditional title of 'visitors') to every monastery. They duly returned with horror stories of debauchery, incompetence and superstition. If the monks had nothing to relate to their discredit it only proved that they were cunning liars. With this propaganda in its support an act was passed in 1536 for the closure of all the smaller monasteries and steps were taken for the immediate demolition of their buildings and the sale of their land. Instinct told people that if such ancient and holy institutions could be so easily, and apparently casually, swept aside that not even their parish churches were safe.

THE PILGRIMAGE OF GRACE

But it was a much more trivial change that transformed this general unhappiness into a massive revolt. For, apparently economic rather than doctrinal reasons, a great number of lesser Saint's Days were abolished by royal decree. On them, instead of working in the fields, people went to church and then had the day off. These opportunities for idleness were thought to be bad for business and bad for morals. (Binge drinking?) A sudden outbreak of inflation that, for the first time for centuries, both greatly increased prices and, in real terms, decreased wages must have increased the general conviction that things were getting so bad that nothing could make them worse. In Lincolnshire first, then in the East Riding and then in much of the north of England the result was rebellion – the Pilgrimage of Grace. After four hundred years of quietly gritting their teeth the people of the East Riding almost to a man rose up and with a vast army marched south demanding that the king must get rid of his 'base and heretical ministers', restore the monasteries and maintain the true religion. These weeks in the autumn of 1536 must have been the most tumultuous and exciting in the long history of these parishes.

Locally the outbreak began at Watton. On the first Sunday of October 1536 the vicar, in giving out the notices for the coming week, failed to announce that October 12th, St Wilfrid's Day, was a 'holy day of obligation'. John Hallam, of Cawkeld, then and now a tiny spot in the parish of Watton -but nearer to Kilnwick than Watton- objected to the omission. The Vicar's explanation that the holiday had been abolished by the king and with the consent of the clergy pleased him not at all. Two days later he met with others in Beverley who were ready for revolt and then 'stirred up Watton, Hutton Cranswick, and all the country up to Driffield and he was the ringleader of them all.'

Similar scenes must have taken place in our villages. Somewhat mysteriously Robert Aske, a lawyer from Aughton in the muddy fields of the lower Derwent, became the leader of this rapidly increasing army. Pontefract Castle, where the archbishop of York and many of the local gentry had taken refuge was captured and soon the victorious host was welcomed into York. The Government was taken by surprise and only a small force could be recruited to block the Great North Road where it crossed the Don at Doncaster. The Pilgrims, with an army, it is said of 30,000 were soon facing the royal army of about 5,000 across the flooded waters of the river Don. But no battle took place. 'The Pilgrims quarrel,' said Aske, 'was not with the king, but with his evil advisers'. The Duke of Norfolk, negotiating in the name of the King promised a full pardon for all taking part in the rebellion, no further dissolution of monasteries and a Parliament to discuss all their discontents at York. With some hesitation Aske agreed to these terms and the Pilgrimage of Grace, with the assurance that they had had some success, came to an end. The army was disbanded and the pilgrims quietly returned home. It had been a busy few weeks.

And, of course, the King had lied. True there was no punishment for the mass of the pilgrims. But unfortunately John Hallam and some others tried to revive the revolt and this gave the king an excuse to cancel the pardon. Hallam, who had made an inept attempt to capture Hull was hanged. Robert Aske, though he had played no part in the revived revolt and had actually met with the king in London was convicted of treason and hanged at York. And for no recorded reason two canons of Warter and the parish clerk of Beswick were also executed. But, rather surprisingly, in the East Riding generally the promised pardon was observed. Nunburnholme, 'the smallest and poorest house in Yorkshire' had been quickly dissolved but with the Pilgrimage the prioress and her sisters joyfully returned to their home. But with the failure of the Pilgrimage they crept away again unpunished for their challenge to the royal authority. It seems unlikely that anyone from Wetwang actually lost his life through taking part in the Pilgrimage.

The failure of the Revolt proved fatal to the surviving monasteries. Despite the Duke of Norfolk's assurances, the alleged support that the canons of Bridlington had given to the Pilgrims gave the king an excuse for the arrest of George Wood, the prior. His conviction as a traitor resulted in the instant dissolution of Bridlington Priory. By the time of his execution at Tyburn on

June 2nd 1537 the Duke of Norfolk had, reluctantly, seen to the destruction of the shrine of St John of Beverley and sent off two great boxes of gold to the king. By next spring the lead (worth £3,000-4,000) had been stripped off the roofs -except for the nave which was to continue as Bridlington's parish church- and the so recently flourishing heart of Bridlington became a desolate and deserted ruin. There followed a campaign of 'persuasion' that resulted in the 'voluntary' surrender of all the surviving monasteries by 1540. Kirkham, surrendered in 1539 was one of the last to go. It remains astonishing that so vast a section of English building, English life and English landowning could be so utterly destroyed in only five or six years.

The King's 'base and heretical servants' (which meant Thomas Cromwell), though they outlasted the monasteries, did not long enjoy the fruits of their victory. Thomas Cromwell was beheaded on the 28th June 1548. Few were sorry.

And, indirectly, much of Wetwang got a new landlord. The next archbishop, Robert Holgate, the former Prior of Watton, felt unable to reject the king's suggestion that he might like to exchange some of his manors for some of the (much less valuable) tithes that had come to the King from the dissolution of the monasteries. So Wetwang, which had belonged to the archbishop for, perhaps, 800 years passed out of his hands.

The Pilgrimage of Grace was an astonishing outburst of courage and energy and faith. And it can claim to be one of the most virtuous rebellions known to history – almost unmarred by acts of violent revenge or the mindless destruction of property. Despite its failure it proved to be a profound learning experience for both the vanquished and the victors. The vanquished- the ordinary people of the north of England- learnt that whatever their numbers they could not by themselves seize control of the central government. This goes far to explain how it was that the rapid changes of religion on the next decades were received so calmly. (A lesson forgotten by the Yorkshire Miners in 1984) And the victors too learnt two great truths. The first was simply that the Tudor state, despite all its grandiose claims, as it lacked most of that machinery of coercion that the modern state takes for granted – army, police, prisons, tax-collectors- in seeking change, must make haste slowly. In the ten years between the Pilgrimage of Grace and the death of Henry VIII in 1547 the worship diet of the people of England would change very little. But in the long run the second truth was to be much more important: for change to be effective and permanent there must be a winning of minds and hearts. That slow process which began in these last years of Henry VIII was eventually so effective that within less than fifty years the great majority of the people of the East Riding had changed from an unthinking but total loyalty to the ways of the old religion to a perhaps equally unthinking but equally total loyalty to the Protestant reformation and a passionate fear and hatred of Popery and Spain.

When Henry died in 1547, despite the rejection of the pope and the dissolution of the monasteries, England was still a 'catholic' country. The services in our parish churches would be almost exactly the same as they had been since the churches were built. With curious impartiality, Henry, in his last years could agree to the burning of protestant heretics and the hanging or beheading of those who would not renounce the pope. But he had taken two decisions that were to ensure a very different future. As late as 1530 Sir Thomas More, as Lord Chancellor had ordered that 'it is not necessary the said Scripture to be in the English tongue and in the hands of the common people'. But the invention of printing had made the widespread circulation of the bible a practical possibility and in 1535 Miles Coverdale's translation of the bible into English was officially authorised. Copies were to be placed in every parish church. It could be argued that this would prove to be the most significant decision that Henry ever made. His second decision was of even greater short-term significance: he allowed Edward, his son and heir, to be educated by protestantly-minded tutors sympathetic to the new ways.

8. THE GENERATION OF CHANGE: EDWARD, MARY AND ELIZABETH

'Catholic' and 'Protestant' are both words that are difficult of definition. If 'protestant' simply meant 'anti-papal' then Henry was certainly 'protestant'. But the key distinction (at least in the 16th century – we live in a more ecumenical age today) was the answer given to that fundamental question 'How can a man be saved ?'

'With great difficulty' was the answer of the Catholic Church, 'but, if you take advantage of the many means of grace given to you by the generosity of God within the life of the church you will make some progress. And if, by the time of your death you have reached, as you must hope, purgatory, then it is the provisions of your will and the generosity of your friends that will ensure that the work of salvation goes forward until you have reached heaven.' Indulgences, the multiplication of masses, the prayers of the saints were all useful and (surely this was psychologically important) gave people something to do at times of anxiety and distress. Increasingly, though, we can see how in the later Middle Ages the busy-ness of our concerns for the dead became the focus of the religious life of the living and something that must have absorbed a great deal of people's very limited leisure and a great deal of such cash that survived the struggle to stay alive.

Martin Luther's answer to that same great question was both the same and also dramatically different: 'with great difficulty and, indeed with such great difficulty that nothing we can do can help us and our only hope of salvation is simply to trust in the loving mercies of our God'. And if we had asked him 'How do you know this to be true?' he would have answered 'First because I found it in the Bible and secondly from my own experience. I have learnt that my utter committment to being a good monk and doing everything the church urged me to do got me nowhere, whilst my faith in Jesus Christ has brought me freedom, life and the assurance of salvation.' A verse from the (much later) hymn 'Rock of ages' sets out this protestant faith very starkly:

Not the labours of my hands

  Can fulfil the law's demands;

Could my zeal no respite know

Could my tears for ever flow,

All for sin could not atone;

Thou must save and thou alone.

Compromise was hardly possible. To the reformers the devotional routines of contemporary catholicism were not picturesque and harmless relics from the past but major stumbling blocks on the road to salvation. The Thirty Nine Articles, first put together around 1542 and still to be found at the back of the Book of Common Prayer make this clear: 'The Romish Doctrine concerning Purgatory, Pardons, Worshipping and Adoration, as well of Images as of Reliques and also invocation of Saints, is a fond thing vainly invented and grounded upon no warranty of Scripture' (Article XXII) and 'The sacrifice of Masses, in the which it was commonly said, that the Priest did offer Christ for the quick and the dead, to have remission of pain or guilt, were blasphemous fables and dangerous deceits'(Article XXXI).

Edward VI was barely ten when he came to the throne. His governments were a rather dubious alliance of dedicated reformers and self-serving politicians. The child-king's contributions to the decisions made in his name must have been minimal but there was no doubt that he was a fervent protestant who grieved at the determination of his step-sister Mary to remain loyal to the religion of her mother. The parishes of England were soon to learn that for them 'reform' really did mean 'change'. These, distinctly shoddy, governments were probably the most revolutionary England has ever known, with a determination to carry through a massive change in the daily living and daily thinking of the people of England with a minimum of consultation.

The Chantries Act of 1547 linked together Government greed and the Reformers dislike of Prayers for the Dead. Most chantries were linked to a particular altar within the parish church. But in the north of England many were in chapels distant from the parish church which had, in effect, become chapels-of- ease to those communities and the chantry priests were able to give significant help in many widespread northern parishes. 'The Chapell of Saynt Katheryn in the town of Tothorpe within the Parisshe of Wherumpercy' soon fell victim to the new Act. Robert Baynton received £4 12s 4d a year to minister 'sacramentes and sacramentals to the parochians of the sayd

Tothorpe'. Even though it was explained that the chapel was more than two miles from the parish church (at Wharram Percy), that there lived there 'xxx howsling people' (adults) and that 'the necessete thereof is to mayntayne prayer' nothing could save Towthorpe chapel. The mystery here is not the destruction of St Catherine's, Towthorpe but the survival of Fimber. It appears on none of the lists of chantry chapels. It must have survived either because of its known antiquity (much older than any genuine chantry chapel) or because, unlike Towthorpe, it had no specific endowment and so there was nothing for the government to steal, or -and I think this most likely- because the Wetwang Churchwardens quietly forgot to remind the authorities of its existence.

Liturgical change came quickly. By proclamation, ashes on Ash Wednesday, Palms on Palm Sunday and the ceremonies of Good Friday were all abolished and 'all the images remaining in any church or chapel' were to be removed. In 1548 a corporate confession in English was added to the Latin mass for those intending to receive communion and then, in January 1549 came the first Book of Common Prayer in English, with an Act of Uniformity that it alone was to be used after Whit Sunday 1549. This book, only slightly amended in 1552, 1559 and 1662 remains today as the authorized Prayer Book of the Church of England and is still in regular use in Wetwang. The aims of the new book are lucidly set out by archbishop Cranmer in the preface. It is still there -with the title 'Concerning the Service of the Church' near the beginning of the Book of Common Prayer and is well worth a read. The service is to be in English, it is going to restore 'the godly and decent order of the ancient Fathers' and the rules for using it are 'plain and easily understood'. The clear hope of the authors of the new book was that the ancient patterns of worship in the parishes should survive. Mattins and Evensong are to be said daily and 'a bell tolled that the people may come to hear God's word and to pray with him' and for Sundays and Holy Days there was 'The Supper of the Lord, The Holy Communion, commonly called the Mass' which, at least at first sight was simply a translation of the old Latin service into English. The priest, as of old, was to wear 'an alb and vestment or cope'. The official emphasis was on continuity rather than change. Yet the new book must have come as a great shock. It was unfamiliar and made the service much longer. Few would have grumbled as the priest gabbled through the latin mass. But not only did the English need to be read slowly so that the people can follow it in 'their heart, spirit, and mind,' as well as with their 'ears' (even today with centuries of familiarity Cranmer's sonorous prose does not lend itself to gabbling), but in an age where many people could not read, congregational participation involved the tedious process of 'saying after me'. None of these changes were popular. There was a big rising in Cornwall where the demand was for the return of all the ancient ways. (They complained that the new communion service 'was naught but a christmas game'). And though Yorkshire, with the memories of the Pilgrimage of Grace still strong, for the most part took the changes calmly there was an astonishing outbreak at Seamer just across the Wolds. There William Ambler and Thomas Dale, the parish clerk, lit Saxton beacon and gathered a 'pious mob' of 3,000 people who denounced 'the laying aside of God's service', and murdered two of those most involved in the dissolution of the chantries. But this protest soon faded out and both were duly hanged.

(Rather oddly, William Amber, in an 1878 book, becomes 'A Celebrity of the Yorkshire Wolds': 'A resident at, and probably a native of East Heslerton who, instigated by religious and political fanaticism, in conjunction with Thomas Dale, parish clerk of Seamer, and others, in the reign of Edward VI raised an insurrection to restore the old Romanist faith and establish a democratic republic in accordance with an ancient prophecy'.)

In 1552 there began what must have seemed a renewed attack on the parishes. Commissioners were appointed for 'surveying of church goodes, plate, jewells, vestments, belles and other ornaments. On the 15th August, Richard Newsome, the vicar of Wetwang and the two churchwardens, John Newlove and Gabriel Marshall, though they must have known that legalised theft was the purpose of the survey, duly sent off their inventory to the local notables-'William Babthorpe, Robert Constable, Ralph Ellerkare, Knightes-who were acting for the government in the East Riding. (Were they doing the dirty work out of loyalty, fear, or in hope of a share of the loot?)

This inventory has survived and gives us a snapshot of the worship in Wetwang church just before this Edwardian Reformation had reached its climax. In 1552 Wetwang possessed 'two belles in the stepill'; 'one challes of silver,parcel gilt'; vestments 'with all things belonging to the same' in red, blue silk, and blue damask, and four old vestments; two copes of 'green dornix'; and one pair of 'sensures' (presumably for burning incense) and a few bits and pieces. Interestingly this is very much the sort of list that a moderately 'high' church in the 20th century could produce.

Copy of
Inventory of Church Goods belonging to Wetwang
AD 1552

This inventorie indented of all the goodes [etc] of the
parishe church of Wetwange, made and certified
by Richard Hewsone vicare theire, and John
Newlane and Gabriell(?) Marshall, churche
wardens, Herry Hogesone and Nicholes Beilbie,
two of the inhabitants of the said parishe, the XVth
daie of August 6 Edward VI to William Babthorpe,
Robert Constable, Rauff Ellerkare, Knyghtes and
John Eglesfeld, esquier. Commissioners for sur —
-veinge of churche goodes, plate, jewells, vestments
belles, and other ornamentes, within th'Estriding of
the countie of York.
   Inprimis, two belles in the stepill.
   Item, one challes of silver, parcell gilt.
   Item, ij copes of grenne dornix.
   Item, one vestment of read saye with all thinges
   belnging to the same
   Item, one vestment of blue silke, with all thinges
   belonging to the same.
   Item, iiij old vestments.
   Item, ij alter colthes, iiij haw l towells.

The 1552 Inventory

Then in November 1552 came the second Prayer Book. This was much the same as that of 1549 except for some significant changes all in a protestant direction: no longer was the Holy Communion 'commonly called the mass', the different parts of the Communion Service were reshuffled to make it harder for conservatives to pretend it was really the same as the old service and no longer was communion to be received with the promise 'This is my body, This is my blood'. The only vestment was to be the surplice.

We can only guess how this ratchetting up of reform was welcomed here. It is possible that the 1552 book may never have been used. For by the end of 1552 the young king was already seriously ill and everyone knew that his fiercely catholic step-sister was the legal heir. The duke of Northumberland (not a Percy!) having married his son to Lady Jane Grey, a devout Protestant, who was third in line to the throne, persuaded the dying king to disinherit his two step-sisters (Mary and Elizabeth) and bequeath the throne to Lady Jane Grey. It was a step too far. A united nation rose up in support of Mary and within nine days the whole corrupt and shoddy structure that Northumberland had tried to erect was swept away. The Catholic Mary Tudor was the undoubted and unchallenged Sovereign of England. The English Reformation was dead and its leaders either in prison as heretics and/or traitors or fled abroad.

Queen Mary was determined to restore the ancient ways. Immediately she abolished all Edward's religious legislation. The clock was back to 1547 and the Latin mass and the ancient vestments and ceremonies came back to Wetwang. It would seem, especially in the north of England, that this was universally welcomed. Going back to 1529 and restoring the authority of the pope caused more hesitation. Did this mean the the return of the monasteries and the chantries ? And what of their lands which a multitude of people had bought in good faith? Mary had to agree that there was to be no undoing of that bit of her father's legislation. And, alas Wetwang didn't get its bell back. Before 1552 there had been two 'belles in the steepil'; thereafter there was only one till a second bell was donated in 1677.

Then things began to go wrong. In 1554 Mary married the king of Spain who thus became the king of England. Not a popular move! Then in 1555 bishops Latimer, Ridley and Hooper and in 1556 archbishop Cranmer were burnt at the stake in Oxford with maximum publicity. This was a massive public relations disaster. The bishops showed great courage as they faced their appalling deaths and people began to realise that these were people of deep integrity and genuine christian faith. Bishop Latimer's last words with their grim gallow's humour – 'Be of good comfort Master Ridley, and play the man. We shall this day light such a candle by God's grace in England as shall never be put out'- proved to be an extraordinarily exact prophecy. In the next three years 1555-8 the deaths by burning of some 300 people, often quite young, purged with fire much of the shabby venality of the protestant years. That no one suffered in the diocese of York was due, either to the good sense of Mary's archbishop or to the fact that were not many convinced protestants in Yorkshire. (But the prebend of Fridaythorpe, having to choose between his prebend and his wife choose his wife and his prebend was given to another) Then Mary and Philip failed to produce an heir. Meanwhile, year by year, the acids of the protestant gospel were steadily eroding the confidence of those who thought the old ways were best. The depression that seemed to mark these middle years of the 16th century was added to, in a very modern way, by a continuing economic crisis caused by massive inflation linked to falling wages that contemporaries could neither control nor understand. Prices rose, the experts tell us, by 50% between 1555 and 1557. *(It might have been caused by the massive influx of silver into Europe brought by the Spanish Conquistadors from their newly conquered South America)*

With Mary's pathetic death in 1558- deserted by her husband and knowing only too well that Elizabeth her heir, Ann Boleyn's daughter, would not be a defender of **her** faith- Elizabeth came to the throne amidst general rejoicing. Elizabeth hoped to unite the nation with a policy of moderate reform.' She did not wish to make windows into men's souls'. Her over riding concern was to preserve the essence of Henry's reform – the Royal Supremacy of the Church. This in practice meant lay control of the church and she would oppose with equal zeal the attempts of Roman popes, English bishops or Calvinist preachers to interfere with that. The 1552 Prayer Book was restored with a few significant changes: no longer did the 'detestable enormities of the Bishop of Rome' get a mention and some of the links with the past were restored -'the chancels shall remain as they have done in times past. And here it is to be noted that such ornaments of the church, and the ministers thereof...shall be retained and be in use as were in this Church of England in the second year of King Edward the sixth.' The vestments, the copes and even 'the sensures' of the 1552 inventory could again be used in Wetwang -though probably they were not. Queen Elizabeth believed that it was possible for people of very differing views to worship together within an agreed unvarying liturgy. Sadly, external events made this policy of total comprehensiveness only partly successful. Europe became locked in a life and death struggle between Catholics and Protestants.

The Spanish attempts to conquer England and Elizabeth's purported deposition by pope Pius V made it difficult for English Roman Catholics to be loyal to Elizabeth and to share in the worshipping life of the national church and difficult too for the government not to see the Catholics as potential subverters of the whole Elizabethan settlement.

Memories of the Pilgrimage of Grace would make the north of England seem a danger area. Inevitably, the prime aim of Elizabeth's archbishops of York was to ensure that the people and parishes of the diocese became good protestants. It would be in these years that all the bright colours of the mediaeval church would be steadily eliminated and replaced with the wholesome simplicity of whitewashed walls broken only by The Apostles Creed, The Ten Commandments, and The Lord's Prayer – with sometimes a bit of splendour around the Royal Arms. In Wetwang some touches of red paint in the crevices of the nave arches are the only reminder of the gaudiness of the unreformed parish church. *(And it is a pity too that the Creed, Commandments and Lord's Prayer which had been gazed upon by generations of Wetwangers are now tucked out of sight in the Tower. It would be good to see them in a more prominent position.)*

The parishioners of both our parishes must have been helped to cope with these extraordinary upheavals by the fact that each had had a vicar who lived through them all. William Marshall came to Fridaythorpe in 1524 and remained there till his death in 1575. In 1548 his age is noted as 46, so he must have been about 73 when he died -a very great age for those days. Richard Hewson was instituted as Vicar of Wetwang on the 28th July 1530 and died in January 1570 -still Vicar of Wetwang with Fimber. These two men, having lived through Henry's break with Rome, the Dissolution of the Monasteries, the Pilgrimage of Grace, the coming of the English Prayer Book, and the sudden return to the old ways with Mary, ended their days in the comparative calm of the reign of Good Queen Bess. If only they had kept a diary! We can't even guess where they stood in the controversies of the time. But there is an explanation of their survival: they, and very nearly everyone else in those days, never doubted that the community in which they lived was a christian community and that its focus was the parish church. Here every child would be christened, every body laid to rest. That anyone would voluntarily separate himself from that community was almost unthinkable. It was only with the passing of the Toleration Acts in 1689 that it became possible for people to contract out of this inherited unity and not for another hundred years, with the coming of the Wesleyan and Primitive Methodists, that the ideal of a single church to which everyone belonged began to fade away. And, of course, if you can choose which church or chapel to go to, you can as easily choose to go to none.

9. PEACE, THEN WAR, THEN PEACE

Consistently, throughout her long reign, Elizabeth had resisted every attempt to change the religious settlement she had made in 1559. The Roman Catholic attempts to overthrow the settlement by force and the 'Puritan' conspiracy to undermine it from within to bring about a more perfect reformation 'after the example of the best reformed churches abroad' (i.e Geneva) were both frustrated. Both sides had great hopes from the new king. The Catholics felt certain that the son of Mary, Queen of Scots, would have more sympathy for them than the daughter of Anne Boleyn. The Puritans were confident that this son of the Scottish Kirk, where the Reformation had been much more radical than in England, would be glad to see his new kingdom move into line in matters of religion with his old. Both were disappointed. 'No bishop, no king' was James' response to those who wanted to complete the reformation in England by the abolition of bishops and the Prayer Book. But James had suffered too many harangues from the leaders of the Kirk to wish to endure the same in England. The results of the King's conservatism were far reaching. For Wetwang it meant another forty years of the Book of Common Prayer. For the Catholics their disappointment led to Guy Fawkes (a pupil of St Peter's School, York), 'Gunpowder Treason and Plot' and a great annual Protestant festival each 5th November. *(This meant not just a bonfire but a service in church 'For the Happy Deliverance of King JAMES I and the Three Estates of England, from the most Traiterous and bloody intended Massacre by Gun-powder.)* The Puritans would have to wait a generation before their ambitions would be achieved – and the price would be a civil war.

With the new century we begin to know a little more about the men who were vicars of Wetwang and Fridaythorpe. Roland Hudson was the first incumbent of either parish to have had a university degree. For reasons unknown in 1601 he agreed to an exchange of livings with Alexander Wolfe who had been vicar of Wetwang since 1570. Wolfe stayed at Fridaythorpe till his death in 1618 – a ministry of nearly fifty years in the two parishes. But Roland Hudson seems not to have been popular at Wetwang. He frequently took his parishioners to law -for not paying tithes, for letting their pigs into the church during prayers, for 'speaking evil of the vicar saying that he grinned like a dog during his sermons'. He died in 1610, and, like many of both his predecessors and his successors, is buried in the churchyard in an unmarked grave.

Interior of Fridaythorpe Church

Richard Neile, who became archbishop of York in 1632, had a different agenda to his immediate predecessors. He tells us that 'out of conscience and duty to God, to King and the most happy Established Church' he was 'a great adversary of the Puritan faction'. Nearly seventy when he became archbishop he was an 'old man in a hurry'. He immediately insisted that the Communion Table be removed from the nave of the church and placed altar-wise at the east end of the chancel with rails in front to protect it. (Dogs were the chief cause of scandal...) We do not know in how many churches the Communion Table had been moved into the nave, thus leaving the chancel entirely unused, but we do know that by 1636 the archbishop's injunction had been universally obeyed, 'even in the peculiars'. In Fridaythorpe church we can see something of the result of the archbishop's campaign. Almost invariably the changes made inside churches between say 1600 and 1800 were swept away in the restorations of the 19th century as they tried to take the buildings back to what they thought they would have been like in the Middle Ages. But in Fridaythorpe church there are some paintings of the church as it was before the 1903 restoration. There we see clearly the Holy Table standing underneath the east window with the altar rail in front of it. And though the chancel furnishings were dramatically changed (not for the better)in 1902, the 1632 (or thereabouts) altar rail is still there, and, of course, still in use.

Thomas Kendall, who came to Fridaythorpe in 1618 after the death of his very aged predecessor, was probably a young man. Certainly he got married soon after coming to Fridaythorpe and is the first vicar of either of these parishes we know for certain to have had a wife.

The Civil War between King and Parliament broke out almost on our doorsteps in July 1642 when the King was prevented from entering the King's Town of Hull. There was even a battle of sorts as near as Cowlam. Scarborough was fought for over and over again and it was Cromwell's victory at Marston Moor near York in July 1644 that made the King's final defeat inevitable. Very many Yorkshiremen fought in the armies of both sides and, both Cavaliers and Roundheads wanted to be on the back of a Yorkshire horse as they went into battle. (Alas, few if any of these animals would survive.) Of how all this affected the daily life of those who lived here we have no idea. It may be signicant that Henry Best of Elmswell's famous Farming Book, written during these turbulent years, whilst giving copious details of the prices of cattle and corn, never mentions politics.

Even Cromwell's victory and the execution of the king did not make as much difference as we might expect. It is true that archbishops and prebendaries were all abolished and their lands sold to pay the costs of the war. But the new government soon proved that they held the rights of property as sacred as did their predecessors. Church lands and church tithes which were in lay hands stayed there. Though the prebends of Wetwang, Fridaythorpe and Holme Episcopi no longer existed Colonel Sandys still collected the tithes. Parliament did dip its toes into the possibility of root-and -branch change. The Parliamentary Survey of 1650 was meant to lead into a major rationalisation of matters like parish boundaries (largely unchanged since the 12th century) and such a redistribution of the resources made available by the confiscation of the episcopal and cathedral estates that there would be an adequately paid 'preaching minister' in every parish. Many sensible suggestions were made: The parish of Wharram Percy was to be abolished. Wharram Percy was to be joined to Wharram-le-Street; Thixendale to Kirby Underdale, Raisthorpe to Fridaythorpe, and Towthorpe and Burdale to be united to Fimber and made into a new parish. But, like many another scheme for change through the centuries, afterwards next-to-nothing happened. As far as I know, none of the schemes for pastoral reorganisation were ever carried through. And though here and there a proper stipend was found for some new 'preaching ministers' no attempt was made to use the funds available to ensure even a modest living wage for the poorest clergy. That had to wait for the Ecclesiastical Commissioners of the 19th century.

The Services in Church, however, did change during the Commonwealth years (say 1648 -1660). The Prayer Book was abolished and its use made illegal. Clergy who were not prepared to accept the new order, or remained supporters of the monarchy were driven out and local committees were formed to ensure the appointment of sound men to vacant benefices. Robert Faucon, the rector of Bainton was the most notable victim of this purge in this neighbourhood. But though the rulers of this new England were united in their dislike of Bishops and the Book of Common Prayer they could never agree on which form of church goverment and liturgy should replace them. So it was left to self-appointed local committees to decide on the shape of the new regime in each locality. This probably worked quite well at both Fridaythorpe and Wetwang for both parishes had 'puritan' incumbents sympathetic to the Commonwealth. The puritan tradition would have been established in Fridaythorpe in 1637 when Francis Sherewood became their very decidedly puritan vicar. It seems unlikely that there was much use of either surplice or Prayer Book. He was also an undermaster at Beverley Grammar School and in 1652 he left Fridaythorpe to become full time Headmaster at Beverley. His successor, William Cooper, though he had been episcopally ordained deacon and priest in 1624 and 1625 proved himself acceptable as 'a preaching minister' in 1650. The record hints that he hesitated before accepting the return of the Prayer Book and bishops in 1662 but he eventually did so and his ministry continued at Fridaythorpe, farming his glebe, till his death in 1686. But he did have some problems: in 1662 Mary Sharp and William and Jane Jefferson seem to have been an active group of Quakers and if they followed the ways of their founder George Fox, they would have been disrupting services in' the steeple house' whatever the way of worship might have been.

Much the same story can be told of Wetwang -but with a different ending. For their preaching minister, Thomas Waite M.A. seems to have been a stronger character than Fridaythorpe's William Cooper. He came to Wetwang in December 1649, after the abolition of episcopacy, and legend has it that it was the length of his sermons that earned him the nickname of 'Old Burnt Roast'. *(I'm not sure that I believe this: did Wetwangers have roast Sunday dinners in 1650?).* But when the bishops came back with the king in 1660 he was not prepared to compromise and was ejected from his living. But his sufferings seem to have been modest. He must have had some good friends and been short of enemies. For, wholly illegally, he stayed on in Wetwang until his death in 1693 preaching twice each Sunday to those who gathered in his house. He and his wife are said to have run a school. This total flouting of all the laws which the 'Cavalier Parliament' had made to prevent such things happening must have demanded a resolute blind eye from those in authority (including successive vicars of Wetwang) and a lack of individuals willing to bring malicious prosecutions.

The collapse of the Commonwealth Regime after Cromwell's death, to later historians has seemed inevitable. But to those living through those early months of 1660 the future must have been very uncertain indeed. And the king's return, to almost universal acclamation and without a shot fired seemed to very many a miracle of God's grace. King Charles II hoped that there could be a reconciliation between the more moderate puritans and the episcopalians but this was sabotaged by both the strong Cavalier majority in Parliament and, or so it seems to us today, the unreasonable nit-picking of some of the puritans. In the end the Restoration Settlement took the line that none of the legislation since 1645 was valid (because it lacked the Royal Assent) and that therefore no new legislation was needed to bring about a restoration of the 'status quo ante bellum'. The last twenty years were simply cancelled. The Prayer Book and the bishops were back and with them came the prebendaries of Wetwang, Fridaythorpe and Holme Archepiscopi.

The last prebendary of Wetwang had died during 'the late unhappy confusions'. The King 'came into his own again' on the 29th May 1669. Astonishingly, as soon as the 13th August he was able to present John Cole D.D. to the revived prebend of Wetwang. And on the 9th January 1663 the prebend, following the ancient procedures, appointed Ralph Wittie, who had been ordained deacon and priest on one day in 1661 to his Wetwang living.

Was all this good news for the people of Wetwang?

In 1660 the churchwardens, Michael Newlove and William Robson, were clearly willing to put the church back to what it had been before 1649 and provide 'a cover for the font, a cloth and carpitt for the communion table, a cup, flaggons and other necessaries.' The 1900 restoration of Wetwang church revealed black lettering on the walls of the transept, (some of which can still be seen) and the date 29 May 1660. So the Rev E.M.Cole may well be right when he tells us that 'in joyful commemoration the parishioners..showed their gratitude by beautifying their church..A similar feeling pervaded neighbouring parishes..At Kirkburn and Wansford commemoration trees were planted.'

Ralph Wittie did not have an easy time at Wetwang. Only three years later he was dead and duly buried in his own churchyard And in those few years he had to take five of his parishioners to court -William Newlove, Thomas Browne,

John Browne, Thomas Stephenson and Joan Bainton – to get the tithes paid on which his livelihood depended and to fight off another court case in which Henry Sandys esq. 'farmer(lessee) of the prebend of Wetwang' was demanding the 'twenty marks a year'(£6 6s 8d) he should pay to the prebendary. All this went back to the arrangements made when the archbishop had 'ordained the vicarage' in 1240. History, in Wetwang, can cast a long shadow.

Matthew Shirt, vicar from 1665 to 1679 is a happier tale. He lived in Wetwang at the Glebe Vicarage opposite the entrance to the church – possibly the last vicar to be really resident until the 19th century. He saw the Church Tower restored and it may have been him, rather than Mr Wittie who brought about the redecoration of the interior of the church. Then in 1677 came the new bell, the gift of the vicar. It bore (and still bears) his name '1677 Matthew Shirt Vicar Venite, exultemus Domino'

People must have hoped that this Seventeenth Century in which forty years of peace had been followed by two decades of upheaval, was going to end with a further forty years of peace. But Charles II's death in 1685 (he was believed to have become a Roman Catholic on his death bed) was followed by the accession of his brother James II – a Roman Catholic convert. Despite assurances he had given, he soon began his campaign to restore England to the Roman Catholic faith. The first step was a Declaration of Indulgence that gave all dissenters -Roman Catholic and Protestant alike – freedom of religion. This was to be read in every pulpit. Seven Bishops refused to allow this to happen. James had them tried before a packed bench of judges who, to his astonishment and the almost hysterical delight of the rest of the nation acquitted them. Never before – and certainly never since – has a bevy of Anglican bishops been so popular. In the years of his exile under Cromwell James (then still in the Church of England) had married the daughter of the Earl of Clarendon and had two daughters Mary and Anne who were brought up 'Church of England' and always remained wholly loyal to that faith. James was nearly 60, much the same age as that at which his brother Charles had died, and the general dismay at the public recognition of Roman Catholicism, was tempered by the hope that it wouldn't be long before his protestant daughter with her protestant husband, William of Orange would inherit the throne. But the widower James II had married the young, Italian and Roman Catholic Mary of Modena and to the general shock, and widespread disbelief, in June 1688 they had a son. This infant, known to history as 'The Old Pretender', was to cost his father his throne. William of Orange, James II's son-in law was invited to England. James lost his nerve and was encouraged to flee to France.

William and Mary with only a shred of legitimate right and that depending on the fiction that James had abdicated and that the new born baby had been smuggled into the Queen's bed in a warming pan, were invited to be jointly King and Queen of England. Hardly a shot had been fired -though it was William's victory at the Battle of the Boyne in Ireland that ended James's hope of recovering his lost Kingdom. William and Mary were childless. When Mary died in 1694 William, with only a modest blood-claim to the throne, (Charles I was his grandfather) ruled alone. On his death in 1702 his sister-in-law Anne,'the Church of England's glory' and the last Stuart monarch began her reign. Most of her many children died in infancy and with the death of the duke of Gloucester before he had reached his teens everyone knew that the queen had no heir. If James, the old pretender and Anne's half brother had been prepared to renounce his Roman Catholicism, I would think it at least probable that the legitimate line would have been restored and the history of England would have been very different. But he would not. The Government, supported by the mass of the nation, was determined that they would never again risk a Roman Catholic ruler. The nearest Protestant heir was Sophia, the Electress of Hanover who was descended from James I's daughter Elizabeth who, having married the Elector Palatinate, had been very briefly Queen of Bohemia before the outbreak of the 30 years War in 1618.

And did all this mean much to Wetwang? Probably not -except for one thing. At the beginning of the new reign there was a renewed attempt to make the Church of England so truly comprehensive that there would be no need for the Dissenters to continue a separate existence. It came to nothing. So the hopes of comprehension having faded, and the new rulers from a Holland long tolerant of a variety of protestants having little appetite for the persecution of Dissenters, toleration became the only alternative. Those faithful supporters of the ejected Mr Waite were no longer risking their liberty when they came to his house to hear him preach. The Wetwang Quakers met in Henry Taylor's house, licensed as a Quaker Meeting House in 1700, had much less to fear than the Quakers of Fridaythorpe a generation earlier.

Modern Historians have often been dismissive of those who called the events of 1688-89 'The Glorious Revolution'. But it can be seen as marking the real end of The Middle Ages and the beginning of modern times. Events had damaged beyond repair 'the divinity that doth hedge a king'. The real rulers of England, until the coming of democracy in the 20th century, became those wealthy nobleman who owned most of the land. The purchasers of the dissolved monasteries entered into their inheritance. The Church too was diminished by the Revolution. When the king was known to be 'The Lord's anointed' there was a dignity in the Royal Supremacy that was lost with a king William and even more with a king George. And as time passed people would soon discover that the bishops, supposed to be their spiritual leaders and guides, were actually chosen, not by the king, but by very worldly poiticians who rewarded them, not for their christian zeal but for their political loyalty. And England really was becoming an Empire with armies and navies and colonies all over the world. Traders and Bankers were becoming as important as Farmers.

So this is not a bad spot to bring to an end this section of our Wetwang Saga. We have told the story of the people who have lived here from the foundation of the village (with a little about the few thousand years before then) until after 1700. The main lesson however has been that nothing much has really changed here in all those years. Houses, Farming, Church were not that really different in 1700 to what they had been in 1150. In the 19th century all that was to change. So you can look forward to another book to take the story from 1800 until today. The Wetwang Saga Part Two is already under way. It will be a better, more interesting book than this. It is going to be written by lots of people working together and it will really try to help you to get to know some of the people who have lived here in the last two centuries. It is something to look forward to.

But as you will have noticed you have not yet reached the end of this book. The pages that follow, under the general heading of the 18th century cover a number of separate subjects that sometimes stretch back into much earlier times and occasionally glance into the future. I am anxious to pass on to you all that I know about these villages and am hopeful that you will find at least some of these 'extra' chapters of interest.

THE WETWANG SAGA:

THE EIGHTEENTH CENTURY

10. BUCKROSE AND BOUNDARIES

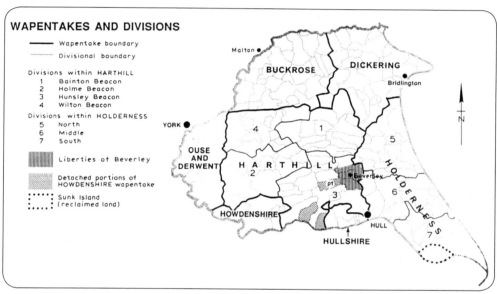

Map of the Wapentakes

No History of England would be complete without something about Buckrose. It is a 'wapentake', a 'deanery' and, presumably a place. The Anglo-Saxons had England divided up into 'hundreds' for the purposes of local government. The Danes, in those parts of England that came under their control, preferred the much more dramatic title of 'wapentake'. A wapentake was the place where people took, or shook, their weapons: a gathering of the local warriors. For Domesday Book in 1086 the North and West Ridings of Yorkshire were both arranged in wapentakes, whilst, rather surprisingly the East Riding, the most Dane-dominated of the Ridings, was still arranged in 'hundreds'. But we soon fell into line with the rest of the county and for the next eight hundred years (or more) most of the East Riding was divided into the four wapentakes of Buckrose, Dickering, Harthill and Holderness. Buckrose and Dickering shared the north, Holderness was Holderness, and most of the rest, from Driffield to the Humber was Harthill. Harthill was so big that in the 16th century it was 'subdivided into five parts, named after the beacons that were prepared to flash the alarm signal across the country should the necessity arise': Bainton Beacon, Wilton Beacon, Holme Beacon, North Hunsley Beacon and South Hunsley Beacon. Through these centuries local government was, to a surprising extent, left to the local communities themselves. But in so far as they were supervised it was done by the Justices of the Peace meeting in the wapentake Quarter Sessions. Government interference in the localities -almost invariably for the purposes of taxation- was also done through the wapentakes. Wapentakes varied greatly in size and Buckrose was amongst the smallest with pleasingly precise frontiers: to the north and west the River Derwent, to the south a line that is roughly the road from Wetwang to York (A 166), and to the east, rather arbitrarily, along the parish boundaries of Wetwang, Sledmere, Cowlam, Weaverthorpe and Sherburn.

And here the ecclesiastic and secular boundaries were co-terminous. The parish and township boundaries were usually the same and the deaneries took the names and the boundaries of the wapentakes. Wetwang and Fridaythorpe were two of the twenty seven parishes that made up the deanery of Buckrose but the peculiarity of peculiars which meant that Wetwang and Fridaythorpe with seven other parishes from the deanery were exempt from its authority must have greatly weakened its significance.

And Buckrose is a place – but we don't know for certain where. The wapentakes took their names from the spot where the 'weapon-taking' took place. Often this was marked with a cross and many wapentake names end with 'cross'. Buckrose is not an exception: originally it is Buckcros. The meeting place might have been in Bugdale near Duggleby, and we are told (Place names of the East Riding) 'there is on the ancient road leading to Wharram-le-Street the base of an old cross which might well mark the site of the wapentake meeting place.'

By the Eighteenth century it was becoming clear that the future was not with Buckrose. It was an area without a town (and the Quarter Sessions often met in Malton) and the growth of Driffield was to make that town the natural centre for much of the wapentake. Then gradually all the business that was once done through the wapentake was transferred to new bodies and the wapentakes drifted into history – almost. But Buckrose had two 'life after death' experiences. The surprising one was the creation, in 1885, of the Parliamentary Constituency of Buckrose. This survived until 1948 when it was divided between Bridlington and Howden. The choice of name was odd for though it included all of Dickering wapentake bits of Buckrose were excluded: Wetwang was in but Fridaythorpe was out. And Buckrose survived, like Harthill, as a Rural Deanery. Harthill, (like Poland) has survived by keeping its name and changing its frontiers. All its southern territory has gone whilst it has succeeded in annexing a good chunk of Buckrose. Wetwang was already in Harthill by 1935, but since then all the six parishes of the Waggoner's benefice have left Buckrose and joined Harthill which is now quite a small Deanery covering Driffield and the area around. A diminished Buckrose struggled on till 2004 when it was swallowed up in a new Ryedale Deanery. For the last relic of ancient greatness you need to visit St. Peter's Church, Norton, where you will find still hangs the banner of the Buckrose Deanery Mothers Union.

11. POPULATION

By chance we have a good idea of how many people lived in these villages near to each end of the 18th century. The Hearth Tax was king Charles II's equivalent of the Poll tax and equally unpopular. It placed an annual charge of two shillings on 'every dwelling... in respect of every fire, hearth and stove therein'. It was invariably called the 'Chimney tax' and was hated because 'it is not only a great oppression to the poorer sort, but a badge of slavery upon the whole people, exposing every man's house to be entered into and searched..by persons unknown to him.' When in 1689 James II was driven out and succeeded by William and Mary, his son-in-law and daughter, amongst the first acts of the new king William and queen Mary was the abolition of the hearth tax 'in order to erect a lasting monument of their Majesties' goodness in every hearth in the kingdom.' But though the tax was gone the diligence of the civil servants of the day (and their successors) has meant that the documentation necessary for the collection of the tax has survived. There it is, still safely in the archives of the Public Record Office. From these documents we can discover not only how many houses (and hearths) there were in every village in Buckrose wapentake but also the name of each householder. The Acts that brought this unpopular tax into being were hard fought through Parliament and amendments were successfully carried that exempted the poorest from the tax. The very poor were not expected to pay church rates and poor rates and such people were automatically exempt from the hearth tax, and there were rather complicated schemes for exempting other poor people also. (It all sounds rather modern). From these documents we learn that Buckrose, in 1673, was 'a poor cottage-dominated area of relatively small settlements... with only five households with over 12 hearths' More than 9 out of ten houses in the wapentake had only one or two hearths. The figures for our villages fit in with this. In Wetwang there are 50 houses; 29 of these are exempt and of the remaining 21, 11 have one hearth, 6 have two and four have three. These four are the big houses of the neighbourhood. No one in Fimber or Fridaythorpe has more than two. In

Fimber there are 16 houses of which seven are exempt. Of the nine who have to pay, five have one hearth and four two. Fridaythorpe has 24 houses of which eight are exempt. But of the 16 houses who have to pay the tax all but two have only a single hearth. Clearly these are all very poor villages. Wetwang is one of very few places where more than half the houses are exempt. But Wetwang is one of the bigger villages in the wapentake, though it is surprising to find that pre-Sykes Sledmere is bigger with 52 houses.

We can only guess what the actual population was. Before the 19th century it was probably smaller than we might expect. Poverty, then as now, could mean a short life expectation and massive infant mortality. If we multiply these households by four we might be about right with 200 at Wetwang, 64 at Fimber and 96 at Fridaythorpe.

Most of the evidence suggests that up till the very end of the 18th century the population and number of households fell in the Wolds villages. From archbishop Drummond's 1764 Visitation returns we learn that by then there were '40 families' in Wetwang and Fimber together and '21 families' in Fridaythorpe. Clergy are notoriously bad at counting heads but there seems no reason to doubt the general accuracy of these figures. So perhaps by then there were less than 200 in Wetwang and Fimber and a bit less than a hundred in Fridaythorpe.

In 1801 the first national census gives Wetwang a population of 193 but it is not clear whether this includes Fimber as well. And the coming century was to see a three fold increase to a maximum of 623 in 1881.

12. WAYS AND WAGGONS

"O Life, how greatly thou hast cheated … how many led astray. A way (via) to life art thou, not Life … And there is no man makes his dwelling in the way, but walks there (nullus enim in via habitat, sed ambulat) and those who fare along the way have their dwelling in the fatherland."

St. Columbanus in about 600 A.D.

Today, our normal manner of speaking is to say that we are 'going by road'. Our forefathers spoke rather of the 'Highway' or more grandly of 'The King's Highway'. This older speech has great significance: a 'Way' means that there is at least a pathway which leads us towards our destination: a 'right of way' is at the heart of the mediaeval and early modern understanding of what we would call a road system. And though there seems to have been much more journeying in past times than we might have expected the few documentary comments that have survived almost invariably refer to attempts to interfere with this right of free passage.

Wetwang is almost at the cross roads of two ancient and important thoroughfares. The Beverley to Malton Road (B.1248) certainly goes back to Roman times: Brough was the Roman ferry crossing of Petuaria and the road went from there across the wolds to the Roman town and fort at Malton. 'Street' was the Anglo-Saxon word for an important and ancient road. 'Wharram-le-Street' makes it clear that this road is that old Roman Road. However, it was only the realigning of this road to bring it into Wetwang at the time of the 1806 Enclosure that gave us the curious double dog-leg that takes the B.1248 in and out of the village. Before then the road went straight across and down through Thorndale to the Tibthorpe Green Lane. The history of the A166 Bridlington to York road is less straightforward but even more ancient. The present main road from Garton through Wetwang to Fridaythorpe is not ancient. But the 'Woldgate' from Bridlington to Fridaythorpe and thence to York along the present road to York is very ancient indeed. It would seem that as long as there have been travellers this was the way they chose to cross the wolds. And this would bring them, from the Sykes Monument onwards along our Green Lane, past Holmfield to Fridaythorpe. In the days of the Stage Coach, the Coach Road from Bridlington to York was via Rudston, Sledmere and Fridaythorpe. The main road through Sledmere used to run a good deal to the south of the present road in front of where the Big House now stands. My guess is that at some point the slightly easier route through Sledmere and past Fimber came to replace the 'Monument to Fridaythorpe' stretch of the ancient Woldgate. This flexibility of route of the now very firmly fixed A.166 does illustrate well the fact that, until modern times, the heart of the matter was that a 'highway' was a right-of-way to get you from A to B and that therefore if it was impassable, for whatever reason, you were legally entitled to make the necessary detour to continue your journey.

With the idea of 'The King's Highway' went that of 'The King's Peace' -not only was there a right of way but travellers were entitled to be protected from attack. In every age the preservation of 'of all that travel by land or by water' has been one of the marks of good government – and a matter for prayer.

Perhaps it is worth noting that, if the proposal for a new Motorway to the east of the A.1 and linking the M.11 to the Humber Bridge and so on to North East England had become a reality it would inevitably have followed the line of the Roman 'Street' from Brough to Malton, and presumably passed in front of Wetwang to the Fimber roundabout. A narrow escape!

We know almost nothing of the thousands of people who have journeyed along these highways through the centuries. The first king Edward spent some nights in the archbishop's manor house at Wetwang as he made his way to the Scottish Wars. (We know, because he signed some charters whilst he was here.) Perhaps the most dramatic (till the tanks came in 1944) of all must have been the passage of queen Henrietta Maria. This was in 1643 during the Civil War between the King and Parliament. She had gone to Holland to sell the Crown Jewels and buy armaments. The weather brought her unexpectedly to Bridlington. 'After remaining at Bridlington nearly a fortnight her Majesty departed for York which city she reached on the 8th of March with three coaches, an escort of eight troops of horse and fifteen companies of foot conveying the ammunition and arms which consisted of thirty pieces of brass and two pieces of iron cannon, with small arms for 10,000 men.'

We can easily forget too the vast numbers of livestock (and geese!) that, in the days before refrigeration and rail or motor transport, journeyed to the towns and cities that could not survive without their meat, in the only way possible – on their own feet. It has been said that Wetwang was a meeting place for drovers. And though the great flocks of sheep on the Wolds were kept for wool as much as meat, the growing population of Hull would welcome many large flocks of sheep. All this livestock was expected to eat its way from the roadside grass as they journeyed and for this the ancient 'greenways' (as their name suggests) were particularly helpful.

The Romans, with the double labour force of their army and conscripted locals built their roads with care – proper foundations, causeways over marshy ground and a cambered stone surface to make the rain run clear. They were built to last. Which was just as well, for it would seem that for more than a thousand years after the Romans left in 410 A.D. the care and maintenance of the highways was not very high on anyone's agenda. That changed in the 16th century when a growing clamour at the dangers and difficulties of travel made Parliament decide that something must be done. The reason for this was partly simply that increasing economic activity meant more travellers. But it was the growth in wheeled travel that was the real problem. The pedestrian, man on horseback, and even the packhorse train could survive the muddiest of tracks. But with the two-wheeled cart and the four-wheeled waggon the situation was obviously very different.

The first 'Act for the amending of Highways' of 1555 with its confirmation and minor amendments in 1563 and 1583 created a road care system that was to last into the 19th century and, indeed, in one important respect, until today. For it made clear that responsibility for the highways rested, not with those who were using the highway, but with the parishes through which these highways passed. And of course 'parish' meant 'parishioners': every adult male had to give six days labour a year (a day was to last eight hours). Furthermore every parish was to elect two 'honest persons' to serve as Highway Surveyors to superintend and organise the work. These arrangements were not as egalitarian as they sound. In most parishes -including Wetwang- the Parish Vestry which was responsible for making these appointments was a 'Select Vestry' that included only 'the better sort' of the parish and it soon came to be generally understood that though the poor were there to labour, the contribution of 'the better sort' was in horses and carts and perhaps the use of their own hired labourers. From the start it was recognized that this was not a very efficient way of getting things done. Even in 1587 it was complained that 'the rich do so cancel their portions and the poor so loiter in their labours that of all the six, scarcely two good days are performed'. None the less the system survived, with some tinkering, until well into the 19th century. The main 'tinkering' was a slow change from compulsory 'statute labour' to a cash payment which could then be used to pay men to do the necessary work on the roads. The change would have been made once for all under Oliver Cromwell when a 1654 Ordinance made it possible for the Highways Surveyors to levy a rate for Highway repairs of not more than 1/-in the £ had not all Cromwell's legislation been automatically abrogated with the return of the king in 1660. In the North Riding around 1800 the 'Statute Labour' system was still the norm and still much criticized: 'the farmer's servant considers this as a holiday; the stone pit will not admit all the carriages to load at the same time; frequently no surveyor attends to direct their work, or keep good order; and if he does attend, he is either unskilful, wants authority, or does not sufficiently interest himself in the cause to perform his duty.' But in Wetwang certainly by the early 19th century a rate had replaced compulsory labour. In 1829, for example, there was a Highway Rate of '9d per £' and the 61 ratepayers together paid £76 14s 4d. The sums paid varied greatly: Jane Wilberfoss paid £8 13s 6d, Walker Field, Peter Knaggs, James Holiday, and John Elgey all paid over £6 whilst ten people only paid 9d with Ann Wilson getting away with 6¼d. The money thus raised was disbursed to a long list of people for 'work done'. In 1835 a reforming parliament finally abolished 'statute labour' and replaced it with a rate. With the coming of County Councils in 1882 the responsibility for repairing the roads was at last taken from the parishes – but the principle laid down way back in 1555 that the inhabitants of the neighbourhood and not the users of the road were responsible for their upkeep was left unchanged. It was going to be different for the Railways!

The Wetwang and Fridaythorpe Surveyors of the Highways must have considered themselves a good deal more fortunate than their neighbours in the Vale of York and around Hull. Their task was to see that there were no obstructions on the Highway and that there was a surface sturdy enough to enable travellers to make reasonable progress. In an area like ours with a chalk base and good drainage this meant finding an adequate supply of flints which were then hammered in to give a good surface. These were found by digging pits into the chalk not far from the side of the road and finding the flints. The only real survivors of these ancient days are the pits left by these centuries of digging. There were six of these in and around Wetwang and traces can still be seen of most of them -the most dramatic is that which is now an allotment where the B1248 turns north for Malton. All are marked as 'chalk pit' except that just outside Wetwang on the Driffield Road which is described as 'Mortar Pit (gravel)'.

The threat to these old and locally-repaired highways lay not with the passage of pedestrians and horses but from wheels. Though – as many iron-age graves have shown – wheels have been part of our human experience for many millennia, it is only in the 17th and 18th centuries that the development of heavy, many-wheeled waggons began to make a new system of road care inevitable. The first waggons came from Holland and the word is Dutch. The outcry against these giant foreign invaders for which our ancient road system was entirely unsuited is curiously similar to that against the juggernaut lorries in the late 20th century. Though some waggons had arrived in Eastern England in the 16th century their spread was very slow till the 17th century. Then they were promptly made illegal! A Proclamation of 1618 "claimed that because of the great weights conveyed by carriers 'waggons' the very Foundations of Bridges are in many places thereby shaken, and the High-wayes and causeys furrowed and ploughed up'. Accordingly, carriages with four wheels or drawn by more than five horses were forbidden." But despite this and much similar legislation by the end of the 17th century, at least in the south of England the four wheeled waggon had replaced the two-wheeled cart as the usual way of moving goods. (Though pack horses were to be a familiar part of English life for another hundred years or more :

'Five and twenty ponies
Trotting trough the dark-
Brandy for the Parson,
Baccy for the Clerk.')

Since these big waggons were clearly here to stay steps had to be taken to save the roads from damage. First came continued -and largely unsuccessful-attempts to limit the weight of waggons and the number of horses that were pulling them. More effective were attempts to ensure that these waggons had broad wheels which were less destructive than narrow wheels. But the real future lay with better roads. Eventually John Macadam, a successful Scottish business man, re-invented (for the Romans had had much the same system) a method of using small stones and gravel to give a road system that was wheel-proof and long lasting. But good roads did not come cheaply and a new way had to be found for paying for them.

These changes came slowly to the East Riding. The archaeologist J.R. Mortimer(he was born in 1825) tells us that in the Fimber of his childhood "The farmers and their wives rode to markets and other places mostly on horseback, the wife often on a pillion seat behind her husband, and often on top of a load of sacks of corn being taken to Malton or Driffield." The day soon after 1800, when a loaded wagon first ventured to make the journey from Fimber to Malton was long remembered as a crowd gathered to see if it could get up that first steep hill on the Malton Road. Way back in 1634 Henry Best of Elmswell was telling his son that to get to Malton market by 9.00 a.m. they needed to leave Elmswell by 3.00 a.m.

THE WOLDS WAGON

Though pedestrians, pack horses and the occasional two wheeled cart were still the main users of the highways in the north, whilst heavy waggons and stagecoaches were already commonplace around London, the distinctive Wolds Wagon had already become a matter of comment by the end of the 18th century. William

The Wolds Wagon

Marshal, reviewing in 1808 a report written in 1796 tells us that "on the Wolds waggons widely distinct in their constructions, appearance, and method of using them, from the common English wagon, may be said to be the only farm carriages in use. But the 'Wold Wagon'(being emphatically so termed) may, I believe, be considered as peculiar to the Wolds. It is, I am informed, the true Flemish or German, wagon. It is guided by a pole, as the coach; not by shafts, as the English wagon. Four horses are usually put to it, very much in the same way as they are to a stage coach. The driver mounts the near wheel horse, and guides the leader with reins; generally trotting, when the carriage is empty; whether in harvest or upon the road."

More than a hundred years later, with their design basically unchanged these 'Wold Wagons' were still an essential, and unique part of the Wolds farm. At Sledmere Mark Sykes saw the military significance of the skills of the drivers of these wagons and eventually persuaded the War Office that a 'Wagoners Reserve' could be useful. Most of the cost came from Mark Sykes own pocket -though the War Office eventually gave a grudging £1,000 towards the start-up costs. The outbreak of war in August 1914 saw the call-up of these reservists and their speedy transfer to the war zones of France. This brought changes both sudden and also far-reaching to the life style of the Wolds villages. The Waggoner's Memorial at Sledmere gives a dramatic and visual account of these events. When the three villages on which this book is focussed -Fimber, Fridaythorpe and Wetwang- were joined with Sledmere, Cowlam and Thixendale to form a single benefice with a shared vicar they had little hesitation in choosing as their name 'The Waggoners Benefice'.

THE COMING OF THE TURNPIKES

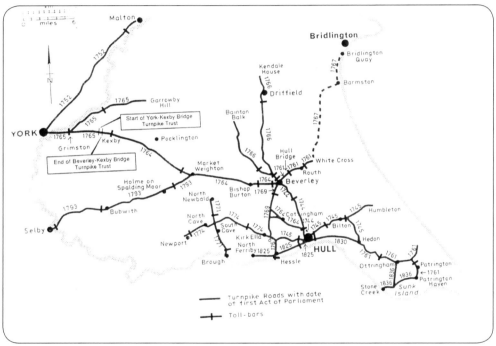

Turnpike Map

Big Waggons and speeding Stage Coaches were worthless without better roads. In many places the centuries-old system of 'Statute Labour' lacked the will, the resources and the technical know-how to bring the roads up to the standards now needed. At the heart of the problem was the fact that, by and large, the roads were now being used for long distance travel and the transport of goods: local people didn't see why they should put themselves out to provide a facility that they themselves would hardly ever use. The argument went – not for the last time- 'let those who use these roads pay for them'. The result, throughout the 18th century was the 'add-on' of the Turnpike Trust. These were set up by Acts of Parliament and gave permission to groups of trustees to raise the money needed to put a stretch of the highway into good condition and to maintain it for the number of years stated in the act. In return they could put a 'turnpike' across the road and charge people for using it. Originally a 'turnpike' was just that -a pike on a hinge across the road that turned to let the traveller past. (Much as it is today in many car-parks). Though the pikes were soon replaced by sturdier gates the old name stuck for these roads and the man in charge of the gates remained a 'pikeman'. That this system of turnpikes was an 'add-on' to the old system is important. The responsibility for their highways given to the parishioners by the 1555 Statute of Highways has never been repealed. We are still paying through our Council Tax. The first East Riding Turnpike linked Hull and Beverley in 1744. 'In 1766 the parson of Hutton Cranswick noted in his parish register that the Beverley and Driffield Turnpike was "set up at Poundsworth Nook on Whitsun Monday in the afternoon being the ninth day of May, 1766". This turnpike in due course earned praise as the best in Yorkshire. Soon there were Turnpikes from Hull and Beverley to York. The route from Beverley to York via Market Weighton and Pocklington was fully turnpiked by 1765 but the route from York to Bridlington was only turnpiked from 'Grimston Smithy to the top of Garrowby Hill'. Similarly the Beverley to Scarborough road was only turnpiked as far as 'Kendale House'(a few miles north of Driffield), and the Beverley to Malton road only as far as Bainton Balk (about where the roundabout is now). In fact there are **no** turnpikes across the wolds. There are two reasons for this (perhaps three): firstly because horse-drawn waggons and stagecoaches found hills very difficult and so if it was at all possible they would find a route without steep hills and secondly because the good drainage given by the wolds chalk meant these highways were passable without the extra expenditure made possible by a Turnpike Trust. Or it could be a tribute to the skills and determination of our Highway Surveyors who did such a good job that there was never any call for a turnpike.

But those who lived here in a turnpike-less Wetwang if they travelled to York would have to pass and pay at the Turnpike gates at either the bottom of Garrowby Hill or at Grimston Bar. ('Grimston' is a bit confusing. It is not at 'North Grimston' but somewhere near the roundabout where the A.165 and A.1109 cross the A.64.) The name is again made familiar to us by the 'Grimston Bar' Park-and-Ride car park.) Milestones were one of the distinctive marks of a Turnpike and the survival of some milestones on the un-turnpiked part of the Driffield -York road suggest that this was a sort of sub-turnpike.

A Fimber Milestone

The Turnpike 'pay -as- you-go' system survived for nearly a hundred years. But after 1840 the coming of the Railways killed road transport dead. Soon the Turnpike Trusts were all bankrupt. The York-Garrowby Hill trust was dissolved in 1871 and all the others in this neighbourhood by 1881. The care of the roads simply reverted to the Highway Surveyors and the local ratepayers and then to the new County Councils till the coming of the Motor Car changed everything!

The coming of the railway was to make one other change to Wetwang's roads. It became cheaper to get limestone delivered by rail than to dig for flints in the old pits. In the old photographs our roads are all blindingly white. And the vestry made a modest income from the rents for the disused stone pits.

BRIDGES

Bridges are barely part of the Wetwang story. I doubt whether Fimber, Fridaythorpe and Wetwang can conjure up a serious bridge between them. (Though there were bridges in Wetwang across the muddy channel that once linked the two pools) But the old East Riding has the River Derwent as both its northern and western frontier. You can hardly escape without crossing water. There has certainly been a bridge at Stamford Bridge since before 1066 for central to the drama of the great Battle of Stamford Bridge was the struggle for the control of the bridge. Was there a bridge in Roman times? But the name 'Stam-ford' means 'Stone Ford' so there must have been a time when the crossing of the river Derwent was made possible by the laying of flat stones across the bottom of the river. The 1066 bridge would have been wooden and certainly it was a wooden bridge that was so dilapidated by 1727 that it needed to be replaced by the splendid stone bridge, designed by the architect William Etty, we see today.

In mediaeval time this Stamford Bridge was guarded by a hermit and a chapel and he would accept gifts for its upkeep.In general the Statute of Bridges of 1531 placed the responsibility for the care of bridges on the local communities in the same way as the Statute of Highways dealt with the roads. But clearly the tiny community of Low Catton in which the Stamford crossing of the Derwent happened to be, could not be solely responsible for the building and maintenance of so vital a part of the East Riding's roads. Bridges soon came to be classed as 'Wapentake Bridges' or 'County Bridges' and in the 18th century the building and care of these County Bridges came to be one of the most important responsibilities of the quarterly Meetings of the Justices of the Peace which was then the only forum for County decision making. The result was some very fine bridges of which that at Stamford- built entirely at the expense of the East Riding-is an early and good example. The signed plans and elevations are still preserved in the 1724 archives of the East Riding Quarter Sessions.

13. WATER – OR RATHER THE LACK OF WATER

Wetwang Mere

Lord Bathurst came to be owner of a good part of Wetwang in the early 18th century. His steward's report on his Lordship's new acquisition, which has happily survived, still makes melancholy reading: " Water is much here wanted; there being only two wells which are at some distance from the Town. The depth of each Well is about fourty yards. There is a pond in ye Town suppl'd only by rain water, wch in dry Summers affords none, and then the Inhabitants are obliged to drive their Cattle three miles for water. The country is open, scarce a Bush or Tree appears for several miles. The Land Stony... The stones upon the place moulder like Lime in ye winter so that no wall

Fence can be made" Not only could much the same have been written about Fimber and Fridaythorpe but the same comments would have been true of each of our villages (or 'townships' to use the ancient and correct term) at any time between their foundation around 1100 A.D and the middle years of the 20th century. Almost invariably people have chosen to build their homes near a river, stream or spring. We have none of these. Instead we have managed with our ancient ponds, some deep and unsatisfactory wells, and the rain from heaven. Why, then, did people choose to live in so unpromising a neighbourhood? The answer, as is so often said, must in the first place be in the soil: the ground was just that little bit more fertile than the average for the neighbourhood. But secondly, I'm fairly sure, it was the existence of the ponds that fixed the actual sites of these villages. Fimber's name itself-originally 'Finmere' the pool amidst the coarse grass'- suggests that this was the name of a place before there was a village there. It has been suggested that the excavations in pre-historic times to create the mound on which the church now stands also created the pools. But this would only have been true if the excavation was of impermeable clay rather than porous chalk. Even if these village ponds owe something to human endeavour they could not have existed if the retreating ice had not left, here and there, layers of clay. I'm fairly sure that it was already existing ponds that resulted in the building of Fridaythorpe, Wetwang and Fimber (and presumably many other Wolds villages) on their present sites. At Wetwang, until modern times, there were two ponds: the top pond was in the middle of the road near to West Field Farm and was linked by a ditch to the bottom pond which was where it is now but twice the size stretching across nearly to Wetwang House. This ditch had a long innings! In 1914 a reporter from the Hull Times grumbled at 'the open sewer which runs from the top to the bottom of the village street' which he found 'most offensive'. And a few years later, in 1920, William Dowson, as an old man writing his reminiscences of Wetwang thought that 'If the channel from the top marr to the bottom marr was covered in, if a few lamps were put in the street for the dark nights, if there was a telegraph office and a good library, Wetwang would be up to date.' It was a strict rule that the water in the top pond was only for human consumption; the animals were to be watered in the bottom pond. (But there is some evidence that the 'top marr' is not as ancient as the, much bigger, bottom pond,)

We know more about Fimber's ponds. Edmonson's generally optimistic 1857 History of Fimber does his best: 'There is also two large Meres situated in the centre of the village renowned for the great quantity of water they contain, but not for its quality, as they derive their supplies from a number of dirty sources, and still the inhabitants allow themselves the use of it.' Edmonson clearly was both proud of, and bothered by, the two Meres. He gives the diameter of the High mere as 52 yards and remembers that in 1821 it was cleaned out leaving a nucleus of dead matter, including drowned cats and dead dogs in the centre of the pond to a height of ten feet. Edmondson was so concerned at the danger to health of this polluted water that he raised funds for the sinking of a well. But this was so little used that by 1900 it had been covered over. J.R. Mortimer, Fimber's other and more famous historian is no more encouraging about the water: 'In springtime the meres became infested with toads and frogs and there were so many lice in the water that it had to be strained through Muslin before it was fit for drinking.' Yet dirty water is better than no water. Fimber's moment of fame came in the dry summer of 1826. Fridaythorpe's ponds were running dry and Fimber at first agreed to share their water. But as the drought got worse Fimber panicked and cancelled the agreement. But the whole of the available male population of Fridaythorpe, with their cattle and water-carts, marched down to Fimber. Fortunately in the fierce fight that ensued, despite broken bones there was no loss of life. And Fridaythorpe didn't get a drop of Fimber's water. And that night the rains came and the drought was over. And I give Edmonson the last word: 'Was it not for bad water, the healthful village of Fimber would be second to none.. the York dale beautiful with evergreens and flowers strewed here and there, and not exempt from the voice of the nightingale at the spring of the year.'

Wetwang's two wells were ancient, very deep and a good way from the village. In Lord Bathurst's day as a curious, but I suspect irritating reminder of the ancient division into two manors 'Peter Liberty pay 1½d p house p ann as an acknowledgmt wch is called Water Banes'. One well was at the bottom of Station Hill and the other down Southfield Balk (which used to be called Well Balk). The deepest well in this neighbourhood (and probably one of the deepest in the country) is at Huggate -339feet. But drawing water from Wetwang's more than a hundred feet deep wells and then carrying it back to the village must have been extremely tedious. These wells had their problems: on July 22nd 1874 there was a Vestry Meeting "to find out the best means for to obtain a supply of good Water for this Parish" and "it was agreed to Bore down in the North Well to see if a fresh or better Spring of water can be obtained." Surprisingly, Mr Dowson tells us that though 'these wells were greatly in use in days gone by, specially in summer time ' by 1920, 'both wells had had their wooden tops taken off and the wells were slabbed over.' A third well in Thorndale has a somewhat shadowy existence: but in 1874 "a Vestry meeting was held for the purpose of taking into consideration the restoring of the Well in Thorndale and making it right so as water may be got therefrom whenever needed – at which Meeting nothing conclusive was come to."

The growing disuse of the village wells was made possible by the increasingly effective efforts of those who lived in these arid villages to save the water that falls from the skies for their own use. Until well into the 18th century the houses of these villages were invariably roofed with thatch. It cannot have been easy to save rainwater from a thatched roof. But once pantiles had become the roof of choice it became much easier to divert the rain water into cisterns adjacent or even beneath the house. Almost every house had its own cistern. At a big farm the water from the farm buildings would be kept for the animals and from the farm house for the farmer and his family. In a modern well organised household the water would be pumped in to a tank in the roof to give water from the taps. These cisterns remained vital until the coming of piped water in the 1930's (1938 to Fimber). As late as 1927 a smart new villa like Milbray (in Southfield Road) was built with its cistern in the ground. In 1929 J.S.Robson's father came to Wetwang as Station Master: 'There was no piped water in the house and drinking water came by train from Garton. The earth closet was in the backyard and a wash house copper was filled with rain water'

Village Pump

One small mystery remains: the 1911 Ordnance Survey Map records a pump next to Wetwang school – and, indeed, several of these pumps can still be seen. When did they arrive ? I've been told that these were a Sykes initiative but that the water for them still came from cisterns filled with water from adjacent roofs.

14. HOUSES AND HOMES

Most of the descriptions that have come to us of the Wolds villages before the 19th century give us a distinctly '3rd World' impression: The houses are single storey, with a thatched roof, low mud or chalk walls, and earth or chalk floors. Sometimes some greater stability was given by building the house round wooden crucks. It would seem that the houses of the vast majority of people on the Wolds in the early 18th century were little different from those of their Iron Age ancestors. There are two reasons for this lamentable situation. The first is simply the almost total absence of worthile building material in the immediate neighbourhood: 'Scarce a Bush or Tree for several miles...the stones upon the place moulder like Lime in ye winter' to repeat the comments of Lord Bathurst's Steward. But stone and timber could be brought a great distance to build a church, a castle or a Lord's house. Why not at Wetwang and these other villages? Because nearly always the landlord was an absentee and the resident villagers lacked the resources to import expensive stone and timber to build a house which would, strictly speaking, belong to someone else.

Not surprisingly hardly any of these primitive houses have survived. There is one mud-walled house in Beeford (which looks quite liveable in) and one cruck house at Octon. Two cruck houses in Fimber were demolished in 1890 and the Revd E Maule Cole has given us an exceedingly detailed account of how these houses were built: 'Two strong curved oak "forks" were reared from the ground, the width of the intended house, nearly meeting at the top, where they were fastened together with short cross-pieces of oak, firmly bolted with oak pins. Other similar forks were raised at intervals of about ten feet, according to the length required. Massive oak beams, resting at either end on oak uprights were then bolted across each pair of forks.... The straw thatch was laid some fifteen inches thick.....A sort of lattice work of oak was then constructed...and covered with clay mixed with straw for a foot in thickness.... As the outer clay walls decayed they were replaced from time to time by chalk stones, cemented with grit.'

J.R. Mortimer's reminiscences of his Fimber childhood gives some idea of what life in such a house was like: 'The barn and stable were at the east end and the cowhouse was at the west, whilst between these, and on the ground floor, were two sleeping rooms, called parlours, and a large room in which the whole family, including the servants, lived, dwelt, cooked and took their food. The only admittance into the dwelling portion of the house was by a narrow passage, called the entry, which ran straight through the building from north to south, between the barn and the house.' The only fireplace would be in the big living room-kitchen. Mortimer tells us that there were seven of these 'long houses' in Fimber. The situation would be much the same in Fridaythorpe and Wetwang. It seems likely that they would for the most part be on the same sites as the 'modern' (i.e. post 1750) farmhouses.

But most people lived in much smaller houses usually called 'nooks' or 'neuks' which have left even fewer traces for the instruction of later generations. Though they were not built until about 1780 (or perhaps 1818) the 'Chalk Houses' (or 'Poor Houses') at Wetwang can give some idea of the past standard of housing for the poor. They were built by the vestry in response to new Parliamemtary legislation to provide accommodation for the aged poor. Rather curiously they were built in the middle of the road near to the top pond. (Presumably this was because the rest of the land belonged to somebody and so was not available for this purpose.) In 1891 they were remembered thus: 'The four charity houses stood on a space in front of the ordinary street houses. They were of one storey, one roomed with a tiny square cubicle jutting out from each. By the side of each square stood a big black water butt containing the house's water supply, the quantity of water being determined by the fall of rain. The houses were very old, built of chalk, and thick enough walls to allow cupboards to be made within their compass.' As late as 1818 the vicarage at Kirkby Grindalythe gives us a glimpse of what many of the old houses must have been like for it has 'only an earthen floor, in which a cottager has a bed, and goes up a ladder into a dark place, where the children sleep.'

The early years of the 18th century were a bad time for the Wolds villages. There was a series of bad harvests which brought about almost famine conditions and a serious outbreak of cattle plague ('the melancholy contagion of the horned beasts'). John Rudd became Vicar of Helperthorpe in 1735. In 1764 he told the archbishop that there were 'About 18 families in all, My Lord, and of these about 10 consist of no more than one or 2 persons in a family. It is a poor village'. Much the same could be said of nearly all the neighbouring villages. Fridaythorpe had '21 families', Wetwang and Fimber '40 families', Wharram Percy (which actually means Thixendale) 18 families and 4 widows.

But in the later years of the century there was to be a great transformation as nearly a century of prosperity crept into our neighbourhood. The underlying cause was the somewhat mysteriously linked Industrial Revolution and the rapid rise in the population of the British Isles. The hungry mouths of the new industrial cities of the North needed food and the East Riding was well placed to meet that need. There was a future for farming and that made possible investment in proper housing for both man and beast. The result was those old houses which still add distinction to our villages. This great rebuilding is usually linked to the sweeping away of the old open fields by Parliamentary Enclosures: 'Parliamentary enclosure provided landlords with both the impetus and income for the building of new farmsteads and eventually the village houses. This was the main period of rebuilding for the East Riding when the old farmhouses and cottages of timber, mud, chalk and thatch were gradually swept away and replaced by more substantial buildings in brick, pantile and slate.' (Pevsner. East Riding p.84) But 'the great rebuilding' had begun in Wetwang -in 1756 probably- some fifty years before enclosure came in 1806.

Woods Farm (in the Main Street next to the Fish-and-Chip shop) can claim to be Wetwang's oldest house. It is built of brick, and this has remained the building material of choice here ever since. It is puzzling why brick was not used earlier. Brick has been known almost since the beginnings of civilisation. (The Bible tells us that the Jews in Egypt were bidden to make bricks without straw.) One of Hull's claims to fame is that 'the brickworks established at Hull c.1303 is one of the earliest recorded commercial brickyards.' The great house at Burton Agnes was built of brick in 1601. When Henry Best built Emswell Hall -barely three miles from Wetwang – in 1635 he had 400,000 bricks made near the site of the house. To make bricks you only need clay. 'The clay was dug out in autumn and left in heaps for the winter weather to break it down.. In late spring it was trodden...to obtain the right plasticity, then moulded into bricks which were left to dry for a month. They were then made into a clamp with turves..and burnt or put into a simple kiln.' There was enough clay in our villages to give us waterproof ponds. It was Garton clay that made possible the Sykes brick works there -the only one on the Wolds- and it remained in business into the 20th century. Much of the building in Wetwang would be done with Sykes bricks and it is this that gives the Main street its pleasing uniformity.

Woods Farm nearly creates the pattern that is almost univerally followed in the century ahead. It has an upstairs -no longer were people to sleep in the ground floor and what must be a distinctly pokey attic; it has buildings out at the back for the animals; it has two chimney stacks giving a fireplace in the main room downstairs and

Woods Farm, Wetwang

in the principal bedrooms as well. In short it is a modern house – and still a desirable place to live in 250 years later. And the only thing that stops it being the perfect child's drawing is that the door isn't right in the middle, and there has been a little bit -also ancient- added on to the front. Look next door at Glebe Farm and though this was built more than a century later it looks much the same as Woods Farm. These were both small farms. Walnut Tree Farm (which is next door again), though it again looks very similar, is in fact much bigger. A wing out at the back makes it a T-shaped building. This was built - probably at the same time as the rest of the house, to house the farm servants. A vast range of farm buildings -that for the most part look of the same age- stretches back almost to Northfield Road. But not all are of brick. Here as elsewhere in the village a number of the farm buildings are built, at least in part, in chalk. Walnut Tree Farm was built in the late 18th century -say 1790.

This must have been a busy time in Wetwang. For the three big farms on the south side of Main Street, Thorndale Farmhouse, Manor Farmhouse and Wetwang House were all, at least in part built at much the same time. Manor Farmhouse, as the name suggests, would claim to be the most important of these. There had once been a stone house in Wetwang. This was the archbishop's Manor House which stood in an enclosure beyond the Mere – where the new Chariot houses have been built. It was the excavations that were intended to find out more about this mediaeval stone manor house that unexpectedly came upon the chariot-grave of the 'Wetwang Princess'. We do not know when, or why, this manor house was abandoned. By Lord Bathurst's time it 'is so demolished that not a Stone is to be seen where it stood.' But some stones from it can, very probably be seen in its successor, the Manor Farmhouse.

The house we see today was built by Christopher Gee, briefly Wetwang's principal landowner, in about 1770. Shortly afterwards, when Wetwang had become part of the growing Sykes estate, Christopher Sykes, though he lived at Wheldrake and his aged father stayed on at Sledmere, used the Manor House as a residential base central to the Estate. Fragments of the various former Manor Houses can be seen in the Church Lane wall of the present house with its unusual mixture of stone, chalk and brick.

But the grandest house in Wetwang is certainly not this Manor House however ancient its roots. This is Wetwang House with its dominant position facing down the road to Sledmere. This was a part of Wetwang that, at that time, definitely did not belong to Christopher Sykes. The Wharram family (who by the vagaries of inheritance became the Wilberfoss family) were proud of their ancient lineage – for after all everyone knew that the Sykes had been tradesmen in Hull only the day before yesterday- and the only family who have ever thought of themselves as Squires of Wetwang. The house we see today was built around 1810 but there must have been an earlier house for the farm buildings have a weather-cock on them with the date 1794 on it. The rise of the Wharrams was seen, legend relates, as a declaration of war on the Sykes. Not only did Christopher come to the Manor farmhouse no more but he had built a new coach road from Sledmere to the bend on the Tibthorpe Road that enabled his escape south without setting even a horse's hoof in Wetwang. The line of the new Coach Road is said still to be clearly visible -but alas not to me.

Thus by the end of the 18th century the bones of the Wetwang we know were beginning to be in place. Gradually the flesh was put on this skeleton by an infilling of small cottages. This was possible because the copyhold tenancies of most of the farms enabled a 'private enterprise' exploitation of spare patches of land by the building of rows of cheap cottages for rent. Many of these were 'meanly built' and many had only two rooms downstairs and two upstairs reached by a ladder. Thus the population of Wetwang could be tripled in fifty years.

The building history of Fridaythorpe is much like that of Wetwang. No really old houses have survived but the framework of 18th century farmhouses (mostly less grand than those of Wetwang) is still with us. The new vicarage of 1796 (now 'The Old Farmhouse') still stands by the gateway to the church, and, again as at Wetwang, the numerous copyhold tenancies facilitated the building in the 19th century of many small cottages.

(Towthorpe, however, which, as we have seen, is an honorary member of our 'Two and a Half Parishes' can justly claim the oldest 'new' house in the neighbourhood. Colin Hayfield of the Wharram Research Project tells us that 'Towthorpe is a 17th century chalk built farmhouse. It was subdivided into two tenanted farmsteads about 1800 and extended. New outbuildings were added and the roof raised to accommodate large new dormitory units.'

As we look around, despite its evil reputation, we find that there are many more surviving chalk buildings than we would expect.)

In both villages by the 1930's many of these small houses had fallen into disrepair. With an astonishing outburst of public spirited zeal Driffield Rural Council condemned most of these small cottages in both villages as 'unfit for human habitation' and successfully demanded their demolition. They then built a square of Council Houses on the edge of each village as a replacement. At Wetwang the gaps this must have left have been gradually filled with new houses but at Fridaythorpe the many empty sites have left the village strangely gap-toothed. And some of the old houses have survived in Wetwang – a few in Main Street and a row of them (the gable windows are new) in Pulham Lane.

Pulham Lane Wetwang

15. LANDLORDS, COPYHOLDERS AND TENANTS

The 'Landlord,' says the dictionary, is 'a man who has tenants or lodgers; the master of an inn'. But the word itself suggests a deeper meaning. In ancient English thinking the king was (under God) the lord of all the land with the privileges, profits and responsibilities that went with that Lordship. That 'Lordship' he delegated to others, and they in turn to others, but there were always circumstances in which the ownership could revert to the crown. And, at least in theory, though the new landlord acquired some of the 'profits and privileges' that came from the land, he also had the 'responsibilities'.

'Tithe' says the dictionary, is 'the tenth of the produce of land and stock allotted originally for church purposes' At first this went to the local resident parson with the pious intention that it be divided three ways between his livelihood, the upkeep of the chancel of the church, and the duties of charity and hospitality. In practice, by well before the 18th century, apart from some small payments in cash or kind to the local vicar, tithe had become another tranche of rent to be paid to the absentee titheowner, who might or might not, be a clergyman.

In these parishes the landlord and the titheowner were almost invariably absentees. But those who lived in these villages, tilled the land and made just enough to feed the family and pay the landlord and the titheowner what they expected were not, for the most part, mere tenants, able to be turned out of their homes at the whim of the landlord. For they were copyholders. **A 'copyhold' says the dictionary, is 'a right of holding land, according to the custom of the manor, by copy of the roll originally made by the steward of the lord's court'.** It came to be the custom of most manors that this gave the 'copyholder' a secure tenure for a number of lives at, probably, a fixed rent. This came to work very much in favour of the copyholder. If the landlord wished to either greatly increase the rent or to get his land back into his own hands he might have to wait till, say, three generations of a family had died. In practice what happened was that when one life was ended an agreement was made to write another life into the copy. A 'fine' (that is a fee) was paid for this privilege and these fines became financially more important to the landlord than the ancient fixed rents. Lord Bathurst's hard headed steward (writing in about 1712) gives us a glimpse into how the system worked -and how hard it would be for a landlord to change it to his advantage! 'The land in this Manr is principaly Copyhold, which Copy holders claim a right of renewal to the next Heir who is presented to the Court... It has been sometimes Customary to put two lives into a copy, but the terms of such renewal being in the Lord's power remains a question. The sum paid upon renewals is about a years purchase; but how far that sum is obligatory on the Lord, seems undetermined, besides the yearly value is hard to become at, by their unmethodical way of computing their estates by the Oxgang. There have been several Copyhold estates renewed, but ye want of the Court Books (Mr Grimstone being absent) and the cautiousness of the people on the place, prevented me from having a particular of that affair.' You can't help feeling a little sorry for the Steward! Eventually the Bathursts gave up on this estate that they had inherited and sold it on. The frequent changes of landlord since the 16th century may not have bothered the copyholders too much.

In Wetwang the list of Landlords is very straight forward until the 16th century. In 1086 Domesday Book records that it belonged to archbishop Thomas as it had to his predecessor archbishop Ealdred. Around 1100 the archbishop gave half of Wetwang to the prebendary. So until 1545 the archbishop and the prebendary shared the ownership of Wetwang, though all the tithes (apart from those eventually allotted to the vicar) would go to the prebendary who, as rector, had the spiritual responsibility for the parish. Robert Holgate, a sturdy Yorkshireman was very much, in the years after the Pilgrimage of Grace in 1536, Henry the Eighth's 'Man in the North'. He received his reward in 1545 when he became the first protestant archbishop of York. But there was a price to be paid: he had to hand over thirty manors to the King. Wetwang was one of them. The King needed money. Wetwang was for sale. It probably changed hands a number of times before in the 17th century we find Sir Peter Apsley Lord of the Manor. Through marriage to his granddaughter it came to the Bathurst family. Allen Bathurst was a Tory member of Parliament for Cirencester till in 1711 he became first Lord Bathurst and a few years later Earl Bathurst. Clearly he was an influential 'mover and shaker' in the times of the early Hanoverian kings. As Treasurer to the Prince of Wales he received a pension of £2000 a year. His son was a Lord Chancellor and grandson Foreign Secretary -who presumably gave his name to Bathurst in Australia. The first earl had fame as a man of taste and a designer of gardens. I fear there is no surviving evidence of his doing much for Wetwang. Perhaps we should be grateful that he did not take his steward's advice that 'one part of this land seems very convenient for a Coney (rabbit) warren wch might be a good improvement' The second Earl Bathurst ended the family's link with Bathurst by the sale of the manor to Roger Gee in 1767. As we will see he took the first step towards the partial enclosure of the Open Fields, but quickly sold the estate to Christopher Sykes in 1774. Inexorably, it seems, the Sledmere Empire is beginning its takeover of nearly the whole neighbourhood.

The cathedrals, with their canons and prebends, were not, strictly speaking, financially affected by the Reformation. So though the ancient link with the archbishop was broken by his 'gift' of Wetwang to the king, the role of the prebendary continued, at least on paper, for several centuries more. Except that it didn't. Edwin Sandys, archbishop of York from 1577-1588, was notorious for his 'nepotism, filling every diocesan office at his disposal with relatives, regardless either of their age or fitness for the posts to which they were preferred.' So his son, Sir Edwyn Sandys, though not ordained, became prebendary of Wetwang. And he seemed to have inherited the financial ruthlessness of his father, for, although he was only prebendary from 1582 to 1602, the Sandys family held Wetwang into the 18th century. Presumably he had leased the rents and the tithes to his son and his heirs with a lease that lasted a number of lives. Certainly in about 1650, when the prebends had all been abolished and their possessions confiscated, the Sandys family still kept a firm grip on the Wetwang (and Fridaythorpe) tithes. The prebend was restored in 1660 with the restoration of king Charles II, but the Sandys still cling on to Wetwang: Hester, a Sandys widow is Lord of the Manor from 1674 to 1690. The Sandys name vanishes in 1699 when Alexander the 8th Earl of Eglinton, having married another Sandys widow, becomes lord of the manor. Lord Bathurst's ever diligent steward tells him that the 'Estate of Peter Liberty' (that is the prebendal estate leased to the Sandys so many years before) has been sold to several persons and if my Lord does not part with this estate, and resolves upon the Improvement hereafter proposed, it may be a proper purchase for his Lordship it being reported that the Estate is now to be sold.' It was in fact purchased by the seventh Earl of Winchelsea in 1734, inherited by his nephew and heir in 1775 and in 1784 sold to Sir Christopher Sykes.

The fields around Holmfield, though for many centuries cultivated as part of the open fields of Wetwang have a slightly different history. Vicar Cole tells us that 'Lands in Holme were given before the Conquest to St Peter's at York.

Archbishop Thomas, who died in 1100, used these lands to endow the prebend of Holme Episcopi, which was then given to the monastery of Hexham. In 1230 it was reacquired by archbishop Walter de Grey. This, like nearly all the other York prebends, survived with its own possessions and its prebendal court until the 19th century. But the prebendal court had authority only over the parish of Withernwick in Holderness and not over our Holmfield. But with the abolition of the prebend, and the death of the last endowed prebendary in 1868 (The Hon H.E.J Howard M.A., prebendary from 1822 -1868) the lands went to the Ecclesiastical Commissioners and were eventually sold to Mr Elgey of Kilnwick Percy farm, whose family had leased the land from the prebendary in 1801 and continued to farm Holmfield until 1944.

For Fimber it is my ignorance (and sloth) that gives us a simpler story. Fimber appears in history as part of the lands of St Mary's abbey at York. With the dissolution of the monasteries these lands came to the crown. It is likely they changed hands fairly frequently in the years of speculation in monastic lands that followed the dissolution. By 1586 the Horsleys, a 'yeomen family' were significant Fimber landowners.

In time 'Horsleys' became 'Langleys' till in 1801 Richard Langley exchanged his Fimber land with Sir Christopher Sykes for some land in Sherburn

St Mary's abbey had never owned all of Fimber and the tithes belonged to the Wetwang prebendary. But by the time of Enclosure in 1806 very nearly all of Fimber belonged to Sir Mark Masterman Sykes. Fimber, for which in 1835 Sir Tatton Sykes paid 91% of the Land Tax (compared to 57% for Wetwang, 20% for Fridaythorpe and 100% for Sledmere) had really become, like Sledmere itself, an Estate Village.

The history of Fridaythorpe's landlords is almost totally different to that of Wetwang with the pattern of multiple ownership established in Anglo-Saxon times surviving until today. To give a complete list of the names of those who have owned some land in Fridaythorpe over the last thousand years would make this a very long chapter indeed. From Domesday book we learn that in 1066 Erneber, Forne and Game had manors at Fridaythorpe, whilst the archbishop had land at Fridaythorpe as part of his Bishop Wilton estates. By 1086 Odo the Crossbowman had acquired the manors of Forne and Game, and the crown held Erneber's single carucate. And somehow the Count of Mortain was including amongst his vast estates 1½ carucates at Fridaythorpe. It is only with the archbishop's estate that we can work out some continuity through the centuries. Around 1100 the archbishop used his land to form part of the endowment of the prebendary of Fridaythorpe.

This endowment was made up of' 5½ carucates at Fridaythorpe, 4 carucates at Goodmanham and interests in Layerthorpe and Tang Hall... It is unlikely that the prebendaries visited or took much interest in their remote estate'. As at Wetwang, after the Reformation, the prebendary's link with his estates was steadily weakened by the custom of giving very long leases to those who, in effect, became lay landlords. Henry Fairfax, prebendary from 1616, leased the lands to members of his family (cf.Edwin Sandys at Wetwang) and they held this lease into the early 18th century. In the 1770's the Duke of Devonshire was the lessee, and then briefly George Hudson 'the Railway King'. After his downfall Lord Londesbrough took over the estate. Throughout the Middle Ages various religious houses -Beverley minster, Kirkham priory and at York, both St Mary's abbey and St.Andrew's priory owned a great deal of Fridaythorpe. At the Dissolution all this land went to the Crown. In due course these were leased or sold to a succession of lay owners. So, after, say 1600, only the vicar of Fridaythorpe survived as an ecclesiastical landowner. When Enclosure came, in 1817, the vicar received 137 acres instead of tithe -and 48 acres as glebe.

But rather oddly, besides this normal survival from the past, in the 18th century ecclesiastical involvement in Fridaythorpe steadily increased. To understand this you must bear with a brief account of **Queen Anne's Bounty**. 'Annates' or 'First Fruits' was the name of an ancient law that the first year's income from a new benefice should go to the pope. In 1534 Henry VIII decided that, as he was now head of the church these monies should come to him. Nearly two hundred years later (in 1704) the distress of the poorest clergy persuaded Queen Anne to return this money to the church. The richer clergy were to continue to pay the 'first fruits and tenths' but the money was to be used to permanently increase the endowment of the poorest livings. The money was awarded in grants of £200 chosen by lot from those whose income was less than £50 a year. When all these had been helped the system went on to help those whose income was less than £100 a year. The winners in the lottery were expected to buy land with the £200 so that the rent would be an addition to the income of the lucky incumbent and his successors for ever. Unfortunately it wasn't always possible to find a suitable piece of land and the £200 was left with the Bounty Board who paid a very modest rate of interest in the hope that this would encourage the purchase of land. By a set of very curious chances this laid the foundations of the Church of England having a central financial authority. Before 1704 the 'Church of England' owned, literally, nothing. All the possessions of the church were actually the possessions, whilst they held office, of the individual bishops and incumbents. From the tiny beginnings of the undistributed funds of the 18th century Bounty Board we have moved to an exactly opposite situation: today the bishops and clergy own nothing: all the church's resources are in the hands of the Church Commissioners and the Central Board of Finance, by whom stipends (i.e.wages) are paid to the bishops and clergy.

And Fridaythorpe, with its multiplicity of small owners was a place where the fortunate beneficiaries of Queen Anne's Bounty could spend their winnings. So by the time of the Enclosure Award of 1817 the vicar of Millington and Givendale had 183 acres and the vicar of Huttons Ambo had 123 acres. The Millington vicar had invested his £200 twice in Fridaythorpe in 1749 and in 1763. On each occasion he was able to buy two oxgangs of land. Huttons Ambo got 6 oxgangs for their £200 in 1742. Fashions change – by the 20th century it had become to seem strange for the vicar to be managing, or even renting out, a 'Glebe Farm' and by the 1940's the three 'glebe farms' in Fridaythorpe had all been transferred to the Ecclesiastical Commissioners who soon after sold them on -usually to the sitting tenant.

Millington Farm

Meanwhile, by the end of the 18th century, Fridaythorpe had been drawn into the Sykes empire by Christopher Sykes's purchase in 1784 of the lease of the prebendary of Wetwang's interest in the Fridaythorpe tithes. This purchase at Enclosure in 1817, gave the Sykes an estate of 258 acres, the largest in Fridaythorpe. After the Act of 1836 had begun the transfer of the possessions of the abolished prebend to the Ecclesiastical Commissioners Sir Tatton Sykes was able to purchase them outright. This may well have made Sir Tatton lay rector of both Wetwang and Fridaythorpe Church. This may have been one of the reasons why Sir Tatton II felt it his duty to take the responsibility for the restoration of both churches.

The Sykes Succession deserves a paragraph to itself. For few of that long list of landowners who have had some considerable responsibility for the life of these villages over about eight hundred years will have ever set foot in any of them or spoken face to face with any of those who actually lived and worked here. Inevitably these centuries of -largely benign- neglect were centuries of gentle decline. By the middle of the 18th century the best hope of much of the Wolds was to be fenced off into giant rabbit warrens. The Sykes changed all that.

This was firstly because they lived in the neighbourhood. Why the Hull merchant Martin Kirkby decided early in the 18th century to move from Hull to Sledmere we don't know. I suspect that the cheapness of the rather barren land of the neighbourhood and the lack of competition -the better off did not think the High Wolds a good place in which to live- were probably the key factors. Martin's daughter Mary married another increasingly successful Hull merchant, Richard Sykes, and in due course, in 1748, their eldest son, another Richard Sykes, inherited the Sledmere estate. One of the reasons that makes it easy to think of the Sledmere estate as a kingdom is the recurring use of the same names. Richard I died childless in 1761 and was succeeded by his parson brother Mark in 1761. He became the 1st baronet shortly before his death in 1783. His son Christopher had been running the estate since 1770 and with the help of his rich wife Elizabeth Egerton of Tatton Park, it had been greatly

The Christopher Sykes Memorial

extended. It was in his time that the Sledmere Estate embraced much of Wetwang, nearly all of Fimber, and a good chunk of Fridaythorpe. On his early death in 1801 he was succeeded first by his eldest son, Sir Mark Masterman Sykes, and then, as he was childless, in 1823 by his second son Sir Tatton. His son, Sir Tatton II succeeded in 1863 and like his father ruled for forty years till his death in 1913. Since then we have had Mark III, Richard II and now Tatton III. Long may they reign!

But as important as this local residence was the family's commitment, through many generations, to the extension and improvement of the estate. Sir Tatton

I's memorial to his father in Sledmere village tells us that "Sir Christopher Sykes Bart., by assiduity and perseverance in building and planting and inclosing the Yorkshire Wolds, in the short space of thirty years, set such an example to other owners of land, as has caused what was once a bleak and barren tract of country to become now one of the most productive and best cultivated districts in the county of York." Much of the change in our surroundings was brought about by the planting of unbelievably large numbers of trees. The determination of the Sykes squires to improve the quality of farming throughout their estate (and so of course to increase its profitability) was made an effective reality through the tenancy system which made possible significant capital investment by both tenant and landlord. And though the tenancies could be ended by a year's notice by either party the custom was for families to farm Sykes land for many years and sometimes for several generations.

Despite dramatic changes in the fortunes of farming (with a prolonged slump from 1880 onwards) the 36,000 acres of the Sledmere Estate remained intact until after the death of Sir Tatton II in 1913. But since then successive sales have seen the empire shrink to a more modest 8,000 acres. Most of the Fimber and Fridaythorpe land was sold in 1941 but there is still a significant Sykes presence in Wetwang. But, rather like the British Empire itself, the heart of the shrunken empire remains strong and in those lands where once the flag flew there remain striking reminders of past greatness. For Sledmere this is a grandly restored church (with a statute of Sir Tatton II tucked away somewhere except at Weaverthorpe where it has been stolen) a school, and in the countryside round about some exceptionally fine farms and a great number of trees.

Copyholders and Tenants: by rights this should be the longest part of this section – for these are, for the most part, the people who actually lived in these villages and cultivated the land through the centuries. The Parish Registers -more or less complete from 1653 at Wetwang and 1687 at Fridaythorpe can give us the names of most of the people living here in the 18th and 19th centuries. Before the 19th century, the Elizabethan Poor Laws – which made the local community financially responsible for all those unable to support themselves – made every village determined to prevent strangers settling in their community. A careful study of the registers would make it possible to work out the family trees of most of the resident families. It would be particularly interesting to find out from how far afield they found their wives. But all this is a job yet to be done. However, a surviving document of 1768 does give a list of 'all the Owners and Occupiers of Lands and Tenements within the Manor and Parish of Wetwang.' This gives us the names of the 24 people who own or rent (or hold by copyhold) the 102 Oxgangs of land which made up the parish of Wetwang. Not all were resident: Roger Gee, Esquire was Lord of the Manor and if he did live in the Manor Farm which he had had built (which seems likely) and look after his 10 Oxgangs himself, he was the only lord of the manor who ever did. 'Christopher Seamore, Clerk' is the curate who looks after both Driffield and Wetwang and, living at Driffield, I doubt if he was the hands-on cultivator of the vicar's two oxgangs. The dominant resident family was clearly that of the Newloves. Simon Newlove (8¼ Oxgangs) and Thomas Wharram (4 Oxgangs) are described as 'two of the principal proprietors'. But we also have eight other Newloves with holdings ranging from John with 11 Oxgangs to Matthew's '¼ an oxgang'. We have both Michael Hardy (3 Oxgangs) and John Hardy (1 Oxgang). And others that seem, almost certainly, to be real Wetwang residents include Francis Taylor (4 Oxgangs), William Hodgson (1 Oxgang) John Robson (½ Oxgang) and John Lundy (¼ Oxgang). Were these people all descended from those 12th century settlers who revived Wetwang after William the Conqueror's harrying? And were they survivors from the descendants of those Viking invaders who gave Wetwang its name in the 9th Century? And how many Viking and Saxon invaders were there? Did the humble descendants of that Iron Age Princess whose body lay undisturbed at the heart of Wetwang for so many centuries simply go on quietly tilling their ground as Romans, Saxons, Danes and Normans passed over them? Earlier scholars did believe it likely that the Anglo-Saxon invasions meant a complete break with the past -and it is certain that the language most of us speak is neither Latin nor Welsh but English. But the dominant view today is that peasants are great survivors. I like to think that the genes of the Iron Age Princess are in the blood of those 18th century Newloves -and so of their descendants today.

16. THE OPEN FIELDS

'**Open Fields**' is the name given to the system of agriculture that dominated most of lowland England (and a good chunk of Europe too) for nearly a thousand years. Oliver Rackham, in his magnificent 'History of the Countryside' tells us that it had "seven cardinal features:

1. The arable of a township was divided into a multitude of strips, the strips of each farmer being distributed either regularly or at random round the township.

2. The strips were aggregated into 'furlongs' and these into fields. The same crop was grown by all the farmers on each furlong. Each field was left fallow -ploughed but not sown- every second, third or fourth year.

3. The animals of the participants were turned loose, to graze the stubble and weeds of all the strips in common, after every harvest and also in the fallow year.

4. The farmers shared some of the labours of cultivating one another's strips.

5. Hedges were few and did not form enclosed circuits.

6. Strips were ploughed in such a way as to form ridge-and-furrow.

7. Regular meetings were held at which the participants agreed on cultivation practices and regulations and fined dissidents."

It would seem very likely that all these seven points were applicable to Fimber, Fridaythorpe, and Wetwang.

It remains something of a mystery how this complex way of enabling a diverse ownership to work together in the cultivation of a village's fields came into existence. It was once thought that this was a system that the Anglo-Saxon invaders brought with them from their German homeland. But excavations at Wharram Percy (and elsewhere) have shown that for several centuries the Anglo-Saxon settlers worked with the same small, enclosed fields that were a mark of iron-age farming. And the new arrangements could not be begun in a piecemeal way. The change was as great, and indeed overwhelming, as the change back to enclosed farms in individual ownership that was to come in the 18th century. Clearly, just as in the 18th century it became generally received wisdom that the Open Fields had become bad news and the progressive way forward was through enclosure, so in the 10th and 11th century the reverse view, mysteriously, became generally accepted. Chewing this over, I've become convinced that the explanation lies firstly in the problem of preserving the fertility of the soil and secondly in the difficulties of getting plough oxen to turn round. Before the days of artificial fertilisers the only way to get decent crops year on year was the careful use of all the animal manure available and a regular pattern of leaving some of the land fallow. Oxen have one advantage over horses for ploughing in that their horns make steering easy. But a team of eight (or even four) oxen needed a very big turning circle. Some open fields were made up of very long strips indeed. With the open fields went the nucleated village. Before the 19th century there were no houses at all in this neighbourhood outside the villages. And as nearly all the villages were on the lower ground where there was a better chance of finding water and shelter, the High Wolds were literally uninhabited. These villages (townships is the old and correct term for them) must have been very close communities indeed. Those who lived in the twenty or thirty cottages and farms that made up the typical Wolds township would be working together and dependent on various common tasks being undertaken by others competently. Sunday would mean being with exactly the same people in the village church ('Chapel' didn't really get going till after enclosure) and a strange face in the village Ale House would be a very rare event. For most of these centuries almost all the needs of these villages – food, fuel, clothing, worship, entertainment- would be met from within the community, or not at all. Fundamentally, the Open Field System had a triple aim: to grow enough to keep the people from starving; to produce sufficient surplus to both satisfy the demands of landlord and church, and, at least in the good years, to provide some cash to pay for that which the village could not make for itself; and to keep the land in good heart for future generations. And clearly it worked. Very nearly every village that appears in Domesday Book has had a continuous existence until today. Neglected land reverts astonishingly quickly first to scrub and then to forest. But we take it for granted that our villages are not islands of good order surrounded by the advancing forest. Where Wetwang's fields end, Garton's and Sledmere's begin. And despite some periods of bad harvests actual famine in these centuries has been a mercifully rare event. The resettlement of villages such as ours in the years after the Norman conquest was a golden opportunity for the new landowners to bring in the new system without the possibility of serious resistance. We know that Elmswell was resettled when it became the property of St Mary's abbey at York. It seems almost certain that that same landlord saw to the new settlement (or resettlement) at Fimber. Similarly there seems little doubt that it was the first Norman archbishop of York who created the new planned and open field community at Wetwang.

"The Open Fields of Wetwang" is the title of an astonishing booklet produced by the children of Wetwang School in 1979. Mr I.S.Spaul's Foreword (He calls himself the 'Series Editor' but is, of course the Headmaster) explains very clearly how the work was done: 'The Authors (C.Henderson and D.Hall) began with the 1855 Ordnance Survey map which gives some of the old field names, and with the Parliamentary Survey of 1647 in which the Roundhead government had written down a list of everything belonging to the Parson of Wetwang. They then began to ask questions - 'whereabouts was this?'- 'how was that arranged?' – 'but what happened if....?' and they turned to the Series Editor for documents in which to search for the answers. The Series Editor duly produced the standard Wetwang documents, which had already been studied by many, many people, and the authors set to work to extract the information they required. They quickly established a basic layout for the open fields, and, as they continued to fill in details, their colleagues working on other aspects of history began to find scraps of open-fields information in unexpected places, in Vestry minutes, in Overseers accounts, and in old Parish Magazines.

When it came to preparing materials for presentation, the authors were anxious that the supporting documents should be, as far as possible, included in this booklet. (This has been done.) When it became clear that pressure of time would not permit the Authors to complete the writing-up and drawing for some aspects of their research, they sat down with the Editor and worked out exactly what they wanted done in those aspects, and the order in which the whole study was to be presented.

I.S.Spaul Series Editor.'

The result of all this work is very impressive, giving us a convincing account of the lay-out of the fields in pre-enclosure Wetwang and of the ways in which they were cultivated. At the same time similar booklets were put together on the Highways, The Poor, The Vestry and the Private Purse of Wetwang. Though these give us many fascinating insights into Wetwang local government in

The Open Fields of Wetwang

the early 19th century they lack that overall grasp of the material which makes "The Open Fields of Wetwang" such a remarkable achievement. My only regret is that Mr Spaul fails to pay tribute to the almost lifelong research of the long-serving vicar of Wetwang of a century earlier, the Revd E.Maule Cole who had not only unearthed these 'standard Wetwang documents' but made them widely available through publication in the Proceedings of the East Riding Archaeological Society and in the Parish Magazine. Presumably similar documents exist somewhere for Fridaythorpe and Fimber but so far, no one has had the patience and skill to dig them out.

Unfortunately 1979 was before the day of the Word processor and the Photo Copier. The rather over-crowded stencilled, unnumbered and stapled sheets haven't worn well. I fear that not many may have survived. But much of the paragraphs that follow comes from this booklet, and it explains why Fridaythorpe and Fimber are somewhat neglected in this section.

The number of fields in an 'open-field' village varied a good deal. Fridaythorpe – with an East Field and a West Field and Fimber -with a North Field and a South Field- made do with a 'two-field' system. Wetwang had the more usual pattern of three fields. This gave a convenient three year rotation – one year fallow, one year corn, and one year a bit of everything else. At Wetwang in the early 18th century 'the usual course of husbandry is to sow one third of ye tillage land with Barley, one third with Oats or Pease, and one third to lye fallow'. The soil at Wetwang was not 'strong enough' to grow wheat. Wolds farmers seem to have been fairly conservative and it was not till the end of the century that they began to grow the new-fangled turnip. Our parishes were unusual in that, at least in theory, nearly all the land had been taken into the open fields where even the dry valleys seem to have been ploughed. But it was more usual for the highest land and the deep valleys to be left unploughed as permanent pasture. All open-field farms had to be mixed for the animals were the only significant source of manure. The average Wolds farmer in 1690 had about 27 sheep but fifty years later this had increased to 71 -but it is unlikely that in these parishes with their limited pasture there were many flocks of this size. But Lord Bathurst was assured that 'Sheep pastures and corn are the only product of that place'. And Lord Bathurst's tenant, Simon Newlove, apparently kept 300 sheep on Wetwang Rakes a rather odd 120 acre patch of Wetwang in the middle of Bishop Wilton. It seems likely that as the flocks increased the proportion of land that was actually ploughed each year decreased. Lord Bathurst was warned that 'a great deal of the Land being very bad, I find is not plough'd in several years'. Arable land on the Wold of Bishop Wilton was 'never sowne above once in tenn or twelve yeares' in the 17th century. In fact much of the Wolds seems to have drifted back into an older 'infield and outfield' system of agriculture in which the manure was kept on the regularly ploughed infields. The names of some of the bits of Wetwang's fields such as High Bitings and Low Bitings suggest that these furlongs (or flatts) were kept for permanent grazing. By the middle years of the 18th century Parliamentary enclosure was on the agenda. Scagglethorpe, in 1725, was the first in the East Riding. Between 1760 and 1780 many thousands of East Riding acres were thus enclosed and the enclosure of Sledmere (controversially) in 1776 brought the new ways to the very frontiers of Wetwang and Fimber. I suspect the surprising decision, made in 1768 'by all the Owners and Occupiers of Lands and Tenements within the manor and parish of Wetwang...for the good of the several proprietors..to agree that certain places called Tussels, Mettils and Short Lings and also..Mettil Cottages should be laid down for a pasture' and 'stocked with cattle' was a compromise to keep the threat of Parliamentary Enclosure at bay. But when Enclosure came in 1806 the new enclosed Cattle Pasture was swept away. Today (April 2007) whilst typing this I look out over those Methils and Tussils (later known as the High and Low Pastures) and see, not cattle, but golden oil-seed rape almost as far as the eye can see.

Mixed Farming meant just that: when Henry Newlove died in 1606 he owned 2 Oxen, 2 Kine, 5 Horses, 4 calves, Bees and Sheep, 14 swine and 'Cocks and Hennes and Durkes'. With, say, a dozen farmyards like this along Main Street Wetwang must have been both noisy and smelly. And with the absence of hedges and fences it is no wonder that lost sheep and wandering geese loom large in our old nursery rhymes. Till the end of the Open Fields era, the Pinder, with the responsibility for impounding animals found where they should not be, was an important village official. The vicar's claim for the tithes of foals, calves, pigs, geese, turkeys, swarms of bees, honey and wax, pigeons and pigeon dung (though there might be some wishful thinking in this list) shows too how very mixed mixed farming could be. But increasingly, in the 17th and 18th centuries it was sheep that really mattered. For it was the sheep that 'grazed the permanent pastures; the aftermath, or foggage of the meadows; the outfields when these were not under cultivation; and the stubbles and fallows of the cornfields. As they grazed they dunged and trod the land, and in most places it was the practice to fold them systematically, fold-bars or hurdles made of willow and ash being used for this purpose. Where pastures were grazed in common it was usual to stint or regulate them.' In Fimber each house had a stint of five sheep in the common pastures.

Sometimes when almost the entire population had gone from a village -by disaster or the landlord's skulduggery – the whole area would be laid down to pasture for sheep or in the 18th century, for rabbits. The Normans brought the rabbit as a carefully nurtured delicacy for the tables of the rich. But by the 18th century two things had happened: the rabbit, having learnt to dig cosy burrows underground, had got tough enough to survive the English climate unaided and the growing hungry masses of the new industrial cities were ready to eat rabbit in great quantities. Much of the poorer land around Wetwang – Cottam, Burdale, and Eastburn- became huge, banked in warrens from which a vast harvest of rabbits was taken to Hull and the West Riding 'in covered carts, containing from six to eight hundred couples strung on rods, and suspended across the cart one tier above another.' The skins were dried before being sold to furriers. But Wetwang, despite the suggestion of Lord Bathurst's gloomy agent that it might be 'very convenient for a coney warren' had, then as now, to make do with the occasional visiting rabbit.

Between them, the Parliamentary Survey of 1647 and The Ordnance Survey map of 1855, enable us to work out, fairly accurately the layout and names of Wetwang's fields and furlongs. The names of Southfield Road and Northfield Road -which are at least a century older than the houses on them – would have suggested that there was a 'North Field' and a 'South Field', but it is not as simple as that! The field to the north of the village was called 'Over Bytons'. Within each field are clusters of strips all running in the same direction -usually north-south, but occasionally east-west- and these clusters make up a 'flat' or a 'furlong'. In 'Over Bytons' these 'flats' are called High Bitings, Isbit Hill, Totter Hills, Short Blealands, Long Blealands, West fields and Bottlands – Burtlands in 1647.(The names come from the 1855 Ordnance Survey map via the 1979 School researchers). The 'Millfield' was mostly to the south of Wetwang. But it gets its name from the long vanished mediaeval Mill which stood just to the east of Wetwang on the south side of the road to Driffield. Traces of its foundations were found by J.R.Mortimer's archaeological excavations. The names on the map suggest that the fields divisions have varied through the ages: Hound Hill, Stand Hills, Scragg Fall, Town Byres, Infield Fall, and Low Pasture. Here too were the Tussels and Methills that were enclosed in 1768. The third field was called 'South Side' and it filled the space between Wetwang and Garton. Its divisions include Low Bitings, Middledale, Wandale, Knowles Fields, North Hills, Heather Fall and Far Fall. Rather confusingly and apparently going across many of these strange names and even the presumed boundaries of the three fields themselves, the 1855 map has the words 'North

Field' and 'South Field'. We also learn from all this that Wetwang was made up of 102 Oxgangs. The name relates to the distance an 'ox' can 'gang': in Wetwang this was thought to be about 20 acres (though opinions differ on this). In practice it doesn't matter for there is something notional about the Oxgang – in reality it is a way of sharing out Wetwang amongst its various owners and residents. If you were down for ten oxgangs it meant that you held about a tenth of Wetwang and could keep ten times as many animals on the common pastures than someone who had one oxgang. Nearly all these boundaries and most of the names would be swept away by the 1806 Enclosure and I suspect that the working out of some of these mysteries is now beyond the memory of man. As important as the three fields was Thorndale- 'a cow pasture of about 120 acres of land; wch Simon Newlove informs me he lets to the inhabitants of the town at Ten pounds p annum and they put in what Cattle they please. It principally bears Gost (Gorse) or whin which the poor people steal and begin to claim a right'. The shortage of permanent pasture was always a problem for Wetwang and the aim of the 1768 'enclosure' was to make this pasture much bigger. Today by walking along the path from the corner of the Huggate Road you come to the only bit of 21st century Wetwang that hasn't changed that much since the 18th century. I hope it can be preserved. Travel a few miles further along that road to Millington Pastures and you can even see something of the past preserved with the long horned cattle grazing on the unploughed, gorse covered, valleys. The loss of this shared use of the common land was the greatest change that Enclosure was to bring. A few lines from a longish and moving poem by the Dorset Parson-poet William Barnes called 'The Common a-Took In' remind us what the common must have meant to the poor. (If you just ignore the Dorset dialect it makes good sense.)

Vor 'tis the common that do do me good,

The run for my vew geese, or vor my cow.

Ees, that's the job; why 'tis a handy thing

To have a bit o'common, I do know,

To put a little cow upon in Spring,

The while woone's bit ov orcha'd grass do grow.

An' then, bezides the cow, why we do let

Our geese run out among the emmet hills;

An'then when we do pluck em, we do get

Vor zeale some veathers and some quills;

An' in the winter we do fat em well
An' car em to the market vor to sell
To gentlevo'ks, vor we don't oft avvord
To put a goose a-top of ouer bwoard;
An' then, when I ha' nothen else to do,
Why I can teake my hook an' gloves, an goo
To cut a lot o' vuzz and briars
Vor heten ovens, or vor lighten viers.
An' when the children be too young to earn
A penny, they can g'out in zunny weather
An'run about, an' get together
A bag of cow-dung vor to burn.

For Fridaythorpe and Fimber, lacking the help of Wetwang's diligent school children, we can recover the names of the different 'furlongs' in their two open fields, but we need a modern topographer, with a good eye for the lie of the land to fit them onto today's map.

In Fridaythorpe's West Field there could be found North Field, Brubberdale Hill, North Dales, and Mickledales. In the East Field were Ladygraves, Middle Caves, Kirk Leys, Skittle Lands, Kirk Holms, and Longlands. In the extreme south-west corners of the parish is a very small cow pasture called Spondhills. Fimber seems to have no dedicated cow pasture at all.

For Towthorpe, however, the diligence of the Wharram Percy archaeologists has given us a survey of the open fields that helps us to visualise what it must have been like in the other villages. 'The whole system is laid out regularly in selions (strips) running north-south, up to 3300ft in length and ignoring the lie of the land.'

THE LOST BIRDS OF THE OPEN FIELDS: DOTTEREL, STONE CURLEW AND THE GREAT BUSTARD.

The Revd W Roberts was Rector of Foxholes from 1895 till 1934. At some point he wrote down, in a splendid copperplate hand his 'Historic Notices of Foxholes'. They begin with these splendid few sentences about the Wolds and its birds:

"Almost within living memory" the Wolds were "little more than a grassy and stony sheepwalk, where it is stated 'a man might ride for thirty miles at a stretch without meeting an obstruction'. In other days the Yorkshire Wolds had a fauna of its own that was essentially characteristic. Vast flocks of dotterel annually appeared and the stone curlew rested on the stony grass grown sheepwalks before they were enclosed in numbers elsewhere unknown. Now (? 1920) the visits of the dotterel are as rare as those of the angels. If a pair of thick knees (local name of the Stone Curlew) are found nesting in some remote corner, the secret is locked carefully in the bosom of the lucky discoverer. But the most notable figure of the Wolds has altogether passed away. Never shall we have the experience of Miss Charlotte Rickaby who tells us that at the beginning of the last century she was riding with her father from Bridlington to Flamborough and she there saw 15 Great Bustards together, giant birds that in the distance reminded the onlooker of fallow deer. It was in 1833 that the vicar of Reighton received from Sir William Strickland an invitation to dine on a great bustard 'the last of its race.'"

The Dotterel Inn at Reighton and more than one Dotterel Farm in the neighbourhood preserve the memory of the vast flocks of Dotterel that used to settle on the Wolds each spring and autumn as they passed from North Africa to their breeding grounds on the Scottish Mountains. The trips were highly faithful to a number of stopover localities and, apparently, "one old haunt near Reighton is said to have attracted gamekeepers from a wide area, prompting the building of the Dotterel Inn to accommodate them." There was such a Dotterel field in Fimber and the historian of Fimber records that after the enclosure of the fields in 1806 the Dotterels never came again. The name was meant to suggest that they were a bit 'dotty' and easily caught. Sadly, being thought of as a great delicacy, in the early 19th century they were hunted almost to extinction.

The Great Bustard was even less fortunate. This great bird -weighing up to 39lbs-and 'at great distance on the open plain presenting much the appearance of sheep' was a nervous and cautious bird that needed a wide open horizon. The enclosure of the Open Fields and the fact that they were very good to eat spelt their doom. By the end of the 1840s they were extinct. But there are still Great Bustards in Russia and Spain and attempts are afoot to get them back to Yorkshire.

Stone Curlews and Great Bustards often live in the same surroundings. Their chosen nesting places are where stony ground has had its grass chewed short by sheep and rabbits. They too found the post enclosure ploughed up sheepwalks no longer to their liking.

17. ARCHBISHOP DRUMMONDS VISITATION 1764

Ecclesiastically speaking the 18th century was not a good time for either Wetwang or Fridaythorpe and clearly a bad time for Fimber. Money was at the heart of the problem. For the Vicar at Wetwang the £24 from Colonel Sandys with whatever he got from his strips in the open fields and the- say £3- the small tithes brought in did not provide a stipend enough for a family man to live on. And the vicar of Fridaythorpe with only £12 from Colonel Sandys and a good deal fewer people to pay the small sums the small tithes would bring in would be even worse off. So each man needed the income from another parish to keep him going and this meant that for most of these hundred years neither Fridaythorpe nor Wetwang had a vicar living in the vicarage.

The last resident vicar at Fridaythorpe, Joseph Richardson (1686 – 1743) was also vicar of Wharram Percy – a not unreasonable link- but thereafter there was no resident parson till the new vicarage was built in the 19th century. **At Wetwang,** for more than a hundred years the parish was linked to Driffield and sometimes to Sledmere as well. Driffield in the 18th century was still quite a small place and the double cure would not be unduly burdensome except that, then as now, wet or fine, Driffield was six miles away. I hope the vicar had a good horse. The chief loser in this was Fimber where for long periods there was only one service a month. The Vicarage Farm would be let. Perhaps it is not surprising that in 1818 the Wetwang vicarage was described as unfit for residence on account of its 'smallness'. Those most involved seemed to find the arrangement bearable: George Colebatch was vicar of Wetwang and Driffield from 1705 until his death in 1755 and from 1715 onwards was 'curate' of Sledmere as well.

In 1764 archbishop Drummond made a formal visitation of his new diocese. The usual questions were asked of each incumbent and their replies have survived. They give a positively bizarre picture of the pastoral arrangements made for the care of these parishes.

At Wetwang Francis Best had been vicar of both Wetwang and Driffield since 1755. At first he may have lived in Wetwang and took one service in each parish every Sunday together with a monthly service at Fimber. Then in 1757 he became rector of South Dalton. As he was the rector he would receive all the tithes and be much better off than he had been with the combined income of Wetwang and Driffield. He now lives in the parsonage house at South Dalton and takes two services there every Sunday in summer and one in winter. But he holds on to both Wetwang and Driffield. 'Christopher Seymour M.A.' he tells the archbishop 'is constantly resident and officiates at Driffield and Wetwang. There being no parsonage house he boards at one Peter Siever's, an honest farmer in the town. The livings of Wetwang and Driffield which have, I believe, generally gone together, amount to between £80 and £90 a year. Mr Seymour receives the whole profits, and we make an equal dividend half yearly. Preaching every Sunday once at Wetwang and once at Driffield, as has been usual, and once a month, according to old custom at Fimber, an old chapel of ease, finds Mr Seymour pretty full employ.' Reading all that nearly three centuries after it was written there is still a smugness about it that sticks in the throat. Francis Best is getting, say £300 a year as rector of South Dalton. Poor Christopher Seymour with three or four times as many people to look after and the endless journeys to and from Wetwang ends up with £45 at best – and out of that he probably has to pay his board to the honest Peter Siever. These arrangements were almost certainly technically illegal (there were laws even then restricting pluralities and insisting on a minimum level of 'duty' in the parish), yet Francis Best outlines these curious arrangements to the archbishop without the slightest hint that it might be thought of as something of a scandal. (Perhaps for completeness sake, I should reveal that Mr Best was also 'curate' of Holme-on-the-Wolds, but as this was a tiny parish only a quarter of a mile from his Dalton church and with a tiny income this might be a forgiveable piece of common-sense. But the fortnightly service at Holme was taken by 'John Wilson, resident curate at Etton')

At Fridaythorpe the arrangements, to our eyes, are even stranger. John Hinde M.A. is the vicar. But he is, 'by your Grace's licence' curate to Mr Blake, rector of Scrayingham ten miles distant from Fridaythorpe, maintaining that the Fridaythorpe house is not large enough for a clergyman to live in. He is able to live at Scrayingham because the rector (who is also rector of Catton) is actually master of the free Grammar School at York and lives there. He takes services at Catton and Scrayingham 'as the season permits' but has a resident curate at both Scrayingham and Catton. Mr Hinde therefore gets £36 a year and a house at Scrayingham in addition to the perhaps £40 he gets as vicar of Fridaythorpe. But who looks after Fridaythorpe? The Revd Thomas Cooper, 'curate to Mr Whaley, rector of Huggate near 2 miles distance from Fridaythorpe. He has £16 per annum with the surplice fees allowed him'. This Mr Cooper apparently lives in the parsonage house at Huggate for Mr Whaley's 'constant residence has been dispenced with by your Graces's indulgence'. Mr Whaley is also vicar of Rudston. Here too he has a curate who gets £25 and lives in the parsonage house. Where Mr Whaley lives I do not know. It seems likely that he has another parish in another diocese. Mr Whaley must have had an income of at least £300 from his rectory at Huggate and vicarage at Rudston. He pays less than £60 to the two curates who do the work. When you unpack this rigmarole you find that Mr Cooper is looking after Huggate (50 families) and Fridaythorpe (21 families) and being paid less than £50 per annum. He must have had a busy Sunday. He takes one service at Fridaythorpe 'where Divine Service has always been performed in the afternoon', whilst at Huggate 'Service is performed twice every Lord's Day with a sermon in the morning'. As before the days of gas-lighting evening services were unknown it is difficult to see how Mr Cooper managed. I hope the archbishop had been told the truth.

The victims of all this were the two curates, Mr Seymour at Wetwang and Mr Cooper at Fridaythorpe and also the two parishes. The curates suffered not only from the smallness of their income but also because of their total lack of job security. Poor Mr Hinde, though his income was not much greater than that of the curates, at least knew that 'the parson's freehold' meant that he would be vicar of Fridaythorpe till he died. The parishes suffered, not only from the lack of day-to-day pastoral care, but also because these visiting curates had neither residence or standing in these communities. The weight of a man's voice in the various meetings by which a village was run depended a good deal on his wealth and his land holdings. These curates would have neither voice nor vote.

But though this picture of church life makes pretty grim reading and we find it hard to understand how the archbishop (or anyone else) found it acceptable, the picture is not wholly black. Unbelievably complex though the above 'arrangements' must seem, they did at least ensure that there was a service Sunday by Sunday in nearly every village and that, whatever his status, they had a minister who accepted that it was his duty to care for the people that lived there.

But there were about to be great changes. At both Wetwang and Fridaythorpe in 1764 the archbishop was assured that there were 'No dissenters'. The faithful band who had gathered round the dispossessed Mr Waite a century before had faded away and even the Quaker Meeting which had once been in Wetwang was forgotten. But in Huggate already '3 families are dissenters commonly called Methodists and one of the 3 families has a licence for his house'. John Wesley made several visits to Bridlington preaching in 1770 'to many plain and many genteel people'. Though his 1774 visit was less successful ('I preached to as stupid and ill-mannered a congregation as I have seen for many years') it was the beginning of a new age for the christian faith in the Wolds. Within a decade (1775 in Fridaythorpe; 1779 in Fimber and Wetwang) Wesleyan Methodism had taken firm root in each of our villages.

POSTSCRIPT: THE SILENCE OF THE LAMBS

The deafening silence through all these centuries has been the voices of the children. They appear in the records that have survived hardly at all. I think they might have been fewer in number than we might expect. For the Open Fields culture with its emphasis on self sufficiency was anxious not to have too many hungry mouths to feed and in an economy that was not looking to expand, extra workers were not really needed. Marriage was probably late and there was strong social and financial pressure against illegitimacy. Did the children go to School and if so where? J.R.Mortimer comments on the education he didn't get from a woman in Fridaythorpe. Perhaps the children were too busy 'getting together a bag of cow dung for to burn'? And certainly minding the wandering animals and poultry in the open fields would keep them busy. We are back to Little Bo-Peep!

18. A LEARNED DISCOURSE ON TITHES, RECTORS AND VICARS AND SOME ASSOCIATED MATTERS. TOGETHER WITH A BRIEF HISTORY OF THE THREE PREBENDS OF FRIDAYTHORPE, HOLME ARCHEPISCOPI AND WETWANG

This portentous chapter heading is a warning, dear Reader, that what follows may not be that exciting. But, as you will have discovered, tithes have had a mention in nearly every chapter of this book. In fact for more than a thousand years, from at least the time that king Athelstan made them compulsory in 926 till their final whimpering away in 1996 tithe has been a permanent cause of division and dispute. It is said (though I'm not sure that I believe it) that more has been written on this than any other subject. But when we remember that the questions about who has to pay tithe and on what, and then again who is entitled to receive tithe and what responsibilities attach to that receipt, have never been finally settled and that paying taxes (and tithe is a tax) has never been a popular pastime, the voluminous documentation that surrounds the subject becomes understandable. But I will struggle to be concise.

Halsbury's Laws of England, (until recently every lawyer's bible) gives a neat definition of tithe :

"Tithes are the tenth part of all fruits, praedial, personal, and mixed, which are due to God and consequently to His church's ministers for their maintenance Tithes are payable yearly out of all things which, with the aid of cultivation yield increase Tithes which arise merely and immediately from the ground, as grain of all sorts, hay, wood, fruits and herbs, are called praedial tithes. ('praedial' comes from the latin word for a farm or estate. Basically these are the 'Great Tithes')

Tithes which arise from things immediately nourished by the ground, as colts, calves, lambs, chickens, milk, cheese, eggs are called mixed tithes.

(Or sometimes 'small' or 'minute' tithes) Tithes which arise from the profits of labour and industry, being the tenth part of the clear gain after charges deducted, are called personal tithes."

Personal tithes, in an age when governments lacked the modern techniques of surveillance and enforcement, proved impossible to assess or collect and soon ceased to be important. The moral obligation to pay them remained and people often left money in their wills to make up for 'forgotten tithes'. This meant that tithe became a land tax rather than a wealth tax and so a matter of especial concern to all those who farmed, or gained their living from, the land. In the Middle Ages this meant the overwhelming majority of the population.

Who paid tithe? Almost everybody. Either the landlord or the tenant would pay tithe on all the produce of the farm and the cottager with a cow and a few chickens would pay tithe on his milk and eggs. There were exceptions. Over the years the areas of land that could claim to be exempt from tithe seemed to increase (a fruitful source of litigation) and the landless labourer, living only on his wages, had nothing that could be tithed.

How was tithe paid? Originally in kind. The tithe-owner's man stood by counting the stooks of corn and taking each tenth one. Some magnificent mediaeval tithe barns still survive. But there was always the pressure of mutual convenience to agree to a money payment instead. But was a 'modus' agreed in one generation, enforceable in the next? Another fruitful source of litigation!

To whom was tithe paid ? The simple answer is 'The Church'. At first what that meant was not very clear – the bishop? the local lord who had built the church and still owned it? the local parson? By the 12th century an apparently straightforward answer had emerged: The rector of the parish, who had responsibility for 'the cure of souls' was to receive the tithe and it was his responsibility to see that some was used for the upkeep of the chancel of the church, some for his own expenses, some for hospitality and some for the bishop. But two loopholes had already sabotaged this simplicity: read on!

Rectors and Vicars. One of the curiosities of the old way of doing things is that, until the 19th century, it seemed to be generally acceptable and normal behaviour to receive a large sum of money for doing a particular job, and then to pay someone else a tiny fraction of that money to actually do the work. Though this was not peculiar to the church, it soon led to the widespread custom of a rich rector paying a vicar or curate very little indeed to carry out that 'cure of souls' which was the rector's responsibility. A 'curate' could be very badly treated. For not only might he have to do a laborious job for very little pay, but he could be dismissed without notice – perhaps his rector had found someone who would do the job for less or had promised the post to the son of a friend when he came of age. A 'vicar' was in a much stronger position. Thirteenth century bishops became increasingly concerned at the neglect of the parishioners that could result from an absentee rector. The word 'vicar' comes from the latin 'vicarius' meaning a deputy or substitute (as in vice-chairman). In 1240 a 'vicarage was ordained' for Wetwang. The rector (in this case the prebendary of Wetwang) was to appoint a deputy, a vicar, who would be supported by a share of the income of the benefice. This was to be fixed and no longer at the rector's whim and the vicar was to have the same security of tenure (the parson's freehold) as the rector- neither could be sacked.

(For completeness sake I should add that there were some incumbents who, though neither 'rectors' nor 'vicars' had the same security of income and tenure. These were the 'perpetual curates'. This rather discouraging title simply meant that their income came from some other source than either the great or small tithes. To encourage them the full description is often 'perpetual curate and titular vicar of x'. Almost invariably these are parishes that have been created in the 19th century or later. Today, however, 'vicar' has become the normal commonly used title for an Anglican incumbent and the word 'rector' has been smuggled into a number of contexts that have nothing to do with the ancient distinctions. Nowadays all clergy get about the same pay. But before the 20th century it is fairly safe to assume that a rector was rich, a vicar middling poor, a perpetual curate poor and a curate very poor.)

There was a traditional distinction between the Great and Small tithes. The rector would get the great tithes – usually corn, hay and wood, and the vicar the small (sometimes confusingly called 'minute') tithes – which, roughly speaking were everything else. The 1240 arrangements for Wetwang and Fridaythorpe were less generous: the vicars were 'to have the cure of the parishes and bear the burdens of the churches and their chapels for ever' but they were to get nothing from 'the lands or rents or tithes of the said churches and chapels'. All that stayed with the prebendary. But the vicar did get 'the tithes of the curtilage' and the 'altarage' (which presumably means the various fees parishioners paid). But in return for this generosity he had to give twenty marks a year (20 x 13s4d) to the prebendary. This settlement lasted, almost unchanged, into the 19th century. In 1662 'Henry Sandys,esq. farmer of the prebend of Wetwang' sued the vicar for his twenty marks and the 1779 terrier (Dict.1. a small dog 2.a register or survey of land) still claimed that 'the tithes due to the minister are the tythe of Hay and Rape and the small tythes as foals, calves, pigs, Geese, Ducks, Turkies, swarms of bees, Honey and wax, pigeons and pigeon dung, whins and carsins'. There had been some change: most of these small tithes had been changed into cash payments – 6d for a foal, 5d for a cow and calf, two eggs for a hen and for milking ewes 6d for twenty. The 1650 valuation shows how unfairly this particular cake was shared : 'The rectory and tythes belong to Colonel Sandyes and are worth yearly £140. The vicarage worth yearly £9.10s'

The second loophole was even more far-reaching in its consequences. This admitted that the 'rector' could be a layman and indeed could be an institution rather than an individual person. A church is 'God's House' and so it is not really surprising that even today it is not at all clear to whom the building belongs. In the 11th century to the man who had had a church built on his ground and at his expense it seemed entirely reasonable that he should own it. And not at all unreasonable that he should recoup the continuing costs of the upkeep of the church and its priest from the tithes he was expected to pay. But by the 12th century this had become a cause of scandal. The great 11th century movement for church reform, which takes its name from Gregory VII, pope from 1073 -1085, stressed the importance of the freedom of the church from any form of lay control. It came to seem blasphemous for a layman to 'own' a church. The dramatic revival of monasticism in the same period solved the moral problem that faced the devout, church-owning layman. He had come to believe that it was sacrilegious (and literally damnable) for him to own a church. But if he gave all the tithes to the local parish priest, who might be one of his serfs, it would make him absurdly rich. That couldn't be right. But to give 'your' church to the newly founded monastery brought glory and fame in this world (together with the promise of prayers for you and your family in perpetuity) and, almost certainly, salvation in the next. This was an offer too good to be refused. Within a generation a very great number of parish churches became monastic property. In due course they 'impropriated' the rectory (and thus gained possession of the great tithes) and granted the small tithes (or part of them) to the vicar they apointed to the cure of souls of that parish. Thus Kirkham priory acquired Garton and Kirby Grindalythe, Guisborough Kirkburn, and, a bit later, Haltemprice acquired Wharram Percy.

One far reaching consequence of this vast transfer of tithes was that of the about 10,000 parishes in mediaeval England perhaps three quarters came to belong to another ecclesiastical institution -cathedral, abbey or college. And this explains why the usual name of the Church of England parish priest is 'vicar'.

And it explains too why, in this neighbourhood, nearly every parish has been cared for, until recent times, by a poorly paid vicar. The only exceptions are Cowlam, -with-a not-very-well paid rector (that is another story) and Bainton and Middleton whose rectors, until the 20th century, were very rich indeed.

Another consequence, inevitably unforeseen by those devout 12th century laymen, was the arrival of a distinctly undevout King Henry VIII, who four hundred years later in 1536 and 1539 suddenly nationalised and closed down all the monasteries and took all their possessions into his own hands. The tithes were quickly sold on to the highest bidder. They were often sold to the local lord of the manor who thus gained a steady income and the right to appoint his local vicar. This massive alienation of a quarter (or more) of the wealth of the church had a number of far reaching results: it created a large class of powerful lay landholders (and receivers of tithe) who were determined to hold on to what they had gained from the dissolution of the monasteries; (even the passionately Roman Catholic queen Mary dared not suggest that they should disgorge what her father had given them); it strengthened the local power of the 'Squirearchy' by giving the squire some control of the pulpit (Jane Austen's Mr Collins had many real life look-alikes); it left many keen church people aggrieved and scandalized at the theft and distressed at the resulting poverty of many of the clergy; and it meant that for the next 450 years, tithes, and all the disputes that they aroused were as much a matter for the property-owning classes as the clergy.

TITHES 1536 – 1996

Legally the Reformation settlements changed nothing in the matter of tithe. But the fact that a tenant farmer might be paying both rent and tithe to the same landlord inevitably encouraged a change from 'payment-in-kind' to payment through a corn rent.

In the 18th century those keenest on improving agricultural methods became increasingly hostile to the fundamental principle of tithe. To these Agricultural Reformers that a tenth of the increased productivity that came from investment in greater efficiency went to someone who had contributed neither finance nor labour to the enterprise was outrageous. The anti-tithe campaign became something like the 'green agenda' of our own day: tithes were a tax on progress. Mysteriously – and to many alarmingly- the population began to increase rapidly in the later part of the 18th century and many believed that it was the baneful effect of tithes that would result in mass starvation. In many parishes – including Wetwang and Fridaythorpe- the decision to enclose the open fields and re-allocate them into individual ownership involved a decision to abolish tithes. Every Enclosure Scheme needed the agreement of the tithe owners. That right of veto gave them a strong bargaining card that could ensure that the compensation they received for the abolition of tithes was not ungenerous. The vicars of Fridaythorpe and Wetwang received a modest allocation of land that at least meant that in about 1830 they had an annual income of £112 and £222 respectively. But Sir Mark Masterman Sykes as the lessee of the prebendal tithes received broad acres that played a significant part in the building up of the Sykes Empire. But the end of tithes for Wetwang and Fimber had come by 1806 and for Fridaythorpe by 1817.

Tithes, however, were still to be part of the history of much of rural England for nearly another two centuries. The Parliament that followed the great Reform Bill of 1832 strove to put right many ancient abuses. The 1836 Tithe Act simply abolished all payment in kind and replaced it with a corn rent that was meant to vary in step with the changing prices of wheat, barley, and oats. As long as the prosperity of High Victorian farming continued this resulted in a generation and more of peace in the tithe wars. (It would seem too, rather mysteriously, that by now the small tithes had drifted into obsolescence. The battles henceforth were over the surviving Great Tithes). But when American imports of cheap prairie cereals led to the unexpected and dramatic collapse of English farming in the 1880's, tithes again became a matter of fierce controversy. The tenant farmers whose rents had been fixed with the tenant responsible for paying the tithes became increasingly unable and unwilling to pay them, and many of the country clergy found themselves in desperate poverty. And at a time when many Non-Conformists were becoming increasingly hostile to the Established Church with a growing clamour for dis-establishment, Methodist farmers found a new reason for not paying tithe to the vicar. (We are told that, strangely there was much less objection to paying tithe to lay owners). Some tinkering with the system and some improvements in farming's prospects eased the situation, but in the 1920's a further farming collapse, after the prosperity of the war years, brought more turmoil. There was a virulent pamphlet war – and it is difficult not to sympathize with both sides. In 1936 the government boldly decided that enough was enough and simply abolished tithe! Those who had been receiving tithes (since 1836 tithe rentcharge) were compensated with an issue of Government stock whose interest was intended to bring in nearly the same income as the abolished tithe rent charge. Those who had been paying the now-abolished tithe rent charge had to pay instead to the government a tithe redemption charge for 60 years from 1936 that was 91% of what they had been paying before. This brought peace in the battle between the church and the farmers but in the long run the tithe payers were the winners: from the start they were allowed to count most of the payment as a necessary expense for Income Tax purposes and then post war inflation would make most of the payments seem trifling. Arrangements were made in 1980 for the ending of the Tithe Redemption Charge and I would think that by the cut off date of October 1996 for almost all concerned it had become but a distant memory. Thus the long contention ceased, not with a bang but a whimper.

POSTSCRIPT 1

The firmly held belief of many that the paying of tithes was ordered by God and that the proof of this was in the Bible added to the fury and energy of these debates. But though the practice can be traced back to the mysterious meeting of Abraham with 'Melchizedek, King of Salem, he was priest of God most High' at which 'Abram gave him one-tenth of everything' recorded in the Book of Genesis, and there are a number of references to the custom of tithing in the Old Testament Law Books it is not easy to deduce from this that God has given the command that all should tithe. But even today, when tithe is no longer compulsory, many christians choose to pay a tithe of their income to the church. Others, however, believe that the poet William Wordsworth's advice

'Give all thou canst:

High heaven rejects the lore

Of nicely calculated less and more' is closer to the teaching of Jesus.

POSTSCRIPT 2

The whole idea of a nationally endowed church has in the last century become so strange as to become almost incomprehensible to a modern controversialist. Most people today consider it an incontrovertible truth that religion is a private concern and that it the responsibility of the believer alone to pay for whatever expenses this may involve. Basically, religion is seen as just another hobby. Indeed from the majority of the plethora of bodies that make grants for good causes, the admission of a religious committment automatically excludes the applicant from any serious consideration. But for the previous millennium it was equally universally agreed that 'the maintenance of true religion' was one of the primary responsibilities of the government. Though it was agreed that the repair of the church building was normally a local responsibility, all the other costs of a resident ministry should come from tithes or some other sort of secured endowment so that the priest, setting 'aside all worldly cares and studies' could devote himself solely to his sacred calling. This endowment of the local ministry was also meant to give the minister a proper independence of his congregation – he was not to be a 'hireling' unable to 'reprove, rebuke, exhort' for fear that his stipend would be cut off. Church of England controversialists were very scornful of the way Dissenting Ministers allegedly cowered under the thumbs of the more wealthy members of the congregation. All this meant that, once so much of the tithes had been diverted or stolen, it was almost impossible to find a way of getting a living wage for the poorest clergy. The 19th century, with its radical transfer of wealth from the cathedrals to the new town parishes, came the nearerst to getting it right. But if we wished to underline one of the greatest contrasts between then and now it is simply that then, everyone (or very nearly everyone) agreed that it was the duty of the state and the local community to support the church whilst now, as Local and National Goverment expenditure escalates to levels utterly unthinkable in earlier ages everyone (or very nearly everyone) agrees that not one penny must be spent on 'the maintenance of true religion' – for that is a private matter.

THE PREBENDS OF HOLME, FRIDAYTHORPE AND WETWANG

The arrangements made by those first Norman archbishops of York to use some of their lands to create prebends that would ensure that the canons of their cathedral were adequately rewarded were destined to remain in place, more or less unchanged, for some 800 years and even today three of the Honorary Canons of York Minster sit in the ancient stalls of those three prebendaries who for so many centuries drew much of their income from the parishes of Fridaythorpe and Wetwang. Though sometimes the personal links of these prebendaries with the place from which they took their name and income are extremely modest it does seem worthwhile to set down a little of the history of each prebend. (I am fairly certain that this has never been done before and will, very probably, never be done again.)

The story of the Holme Prebend can be brief. The name came from the small village of Holme within the parish of Wetwang. Though the village was abandoned in the Middle Ages and its fields quietly absorbed into those of Wetwang, it always remained a separate estate in the archbishop's books and has maintained that separateness into modern times. Soon after the creation of the prebend in the 12th century the archbishop gave it to Hexham abbey (then within a detached part of York diocese) but in 1230, Walter de Gray, a very organising archbishop, restored it to York and modestly increased its wealth by adding the parish of Withernwick in remote Holderness, to the prebend.

This had belonged to the abbey of Aumale in France – no doubt through the generosity of the Counts of Aumale who ruled in Holderness from 1086 until 1260. It must have been an incident in the not untroubled history of the Count's relationships with the kings of England that brought Withernwick to the archbishop of York and so to the prebendary of Holme. With Withernwick Holme acquired its own peculiar court which almost certainly the smallest juridsdiction of any. And Withernwick stepped into the Liberty of St Peter. The poorest of our three prebends it was worth £16 13s 4d in 1245 and £11 16s 0½d in 1535.

On Fridaythorpe we can be even shorter. Though the Fridaythorpe prebendary held land in this village he was always only one of a number of landowners and his main income came from Tang on the outskirts of York. Ecclesiastically Fridaythorpe belonged to the Wetwang prebend. In 1245 it was worth £40 and in 1535 £38 16s 0½d

Wetwang became a very wealthy prebend. Worth £128 in 1245, though, mysteriously, by 1535 it had shrunk to £80 11s 3d it was still the richest of the York prebends. It had interests not only in Wetwang and Fridaythorpe but also in Elloughton, Kirby Wharfe and Ulleskelfe and all these places were under the authority of the Wetwang Peculiar Court. At Wetwang there was a prebendal house (probably next to the church where Coates Farm is now) with a tithe barn. This wealth made it a much sought after preferment. Cardinal Wolsey, who became archbishop of York in 1514, first gave the prebend to his illegitimate son and then, in 1528, gained a papal bull that transferred the prebend to his newly founded Cardinal's College at Oxford. After the Cardinal's downfall, the college became first King Henry VIII's College and then Christchurch, and it looked likely that with royal support, it would keep its grasp on the Wetwang prebend. But, mysteriously, by 1557 it was safely back in the gift of the archbishop (Wetwang might have been better off if it had stayed with Christchurch. They might have made sure that as a 'college living' the incumbent, who would usually have been one of their fellows, got a proper stipend.)

The vicars of both Wetwang and Fridaythorpe lived through the astonishing changes of the Reformation years unscathed. But the accession of the protestant queen Elizabeth was a change too many for George Palmes who was deprived of the Wetwang prebend in 1559 for his refusal to subscribe to the Act of Supremacy. (This 'catholic martyr' balances the 'protestant' Henry Williams who was deprived of his Fridaythorpe prebend by queen Mary for refusing to put away his wife.)

In 1582 Edwin Sandys, a son of the archbishop and a layman was given the prebend. He seems to have succeeded in so arranging the leasing of the prebendal lands and tithes that to all intents and purposes they became the possession of the Sandys family for more than a hundred years. By the 18th century, though the prebendal legal status and wealth was unchanged, in reality these lands had been secularised and could be bought and sold much the same as other land. This made it possible for the Sykes family to gain control of the prebendal lands and tithes in both Fridaythorpe and Wetwang even though, technically, the prebendaries still owned them.

These sinecure canonries (or prebends) had never been popular with the general public and even ardent church apologists found it difficult to justify the payment of large salaries to people who had nothing very much to do. A 17th century critic described the cathedrals as 'dens of loitering lubbers' and with the coming of Oliver Cromwell the whole cathedral establishment was swept away. But with the king's return the old ways were instantly restored: 1660 saw the return of Henry Fairfax to his Fridaythorpe prebend and fresh appointments to Holme and Wetwang.

But by the 1830's the demand for the reform of old abuses that was sweeping the country could not ignore some of the ancient scandals that so weakened the Established Church. To many, the scandal was not so much that some clergy were rich and possibly idle but that in many of the vast new towns and cities being created by the Industrial Revolution there were no clergy at all. An Ecclesiastical Commission set up in 1835 was appalled at the spiritual neglect it uncovered and realistic in its recognition both, that money must be found to provide churches and clergy for these new areas and that there was no possibility of this money being found from the government or the general public as long as there were vast resources being misused within the church. With astonishing ruthlessness the Commission (which was mostly nade up of bishops) brought to Parliament a Chapters Bill which radically reformed the cathedrals: all sinecure prebends and canonries were to be suppressed and, with very few exceptions there were to be no more than four residentiary canonries in each cathedral. The outrage of the cathedrals was immense. They argued, not entirely unjustly, that they were being robbed so that episcopal wealth could be preserved intact. But by 1840 the Bill had become an Act of Parliament, the prebends of Holme, Fridaythorpe and Wetwang were no more, and the modern history of the Church of England had begun.

Nearly but not quite yet! The corpse was to go on twitching for a few years yet. For that all-important Chapters Act included two concessions to the cathedrals lobby – one inevitable and the other, I think, misguided. It was inevitable, as prebends were property, that the rights of existing office-holders should be protected. Nothing was to change until the current prebendary had resigned or died. And clergy, especially those with a point of principle to prove, can live a very long time indeed. Misguided however, was the attempt to ease the shock of the change by allowing every third vacancy to be filled. It was going to be some time before all the resources tied up in the old system were to be available for the benefit of the new.

Then the Chapters Act contained a surprising and forward looking clause for the creation of 'Honorary Canonries' in every cathedral. They were to be entirely unpaid and in the gift of the bishop. Though these new honorary canons usually had some modest role in the life of the cathedral, they were really meant to preserve one of the good things within the old regime. An appointment to a canonry could be a mark of respect offered by the bishop to some hard working priest who had spent a lifetime in difficult parishes without any very obvious reward. To many of the clergy being made a canon means a great deal – and it can be even more welcomed by their wives. Today (2008) the Revd Canon Edward Newlyn, the Revd Canon Kate Goulder and the Revd Canon Valerie Hewitson are prebendaries, respectively, of Fridaythorpe, Holme Archepiscopi, and Wetwang.

This has been a tough journey. But if you have stuck with it to the end at least you will be able to read Jane Austen and Anthony Trollope with a greater understanding of the antics and attitudes of the clergy. The perpetual curate of Hogglestock is less to be envied than the rector of Plumstead Episcopi.

SOME FURTHER READING THAT MIGHT BE HELPFUL

Victoria County History Vol VIII. East Buckrose: Sledmere and the Northern Wolds. D & S Neave 2008
> This gives you, succintly, all the basic facts.

The North of England. A History Frank Musgrove 1990 Blackwell

An Historical Atlas of East Yorkshire S Neave & S Ellis 1996
> A mine of useful information clearly presented

Ebor: A History of the Archbishops of York A Tindal Hart 1986

The Rural Landscape of the East Riding of Yorkshire 1700-1850
> Alan Harris 1961 O.U.P

The East Riding of Yorkshire Landscape K.J.Allison 1976

The Forgotten Landscapes of the Yorkshire Wolds
> Chris Fenton-Thomas 2005 Tempus
> This is very good on the Green Lanes

The History of The Countryside Oliver Rackham 1986
> This is one of those great books which really does tell you everything you want to know.

Britain B.C. and **Britain A.D.** Frances Pryor 2003 Harper Collins
> These two books give a clear and comprehensive account of what happened up to the Anglo-Saxons

Churches in the Landscape Richard Morris 1989 Phoenix
> This takes the history of our church buildings way back into Anglo-Saxon times

Domesday Book The full text in modern English 2002 Penguin

The Black Death Philip Ziegler 1969. A fascinating read

The Black Death Ole Benedictow 2004.
This is very learned -but in the end you will know everything there is to know about the subject.

The Peasants' Revolt Alastair Dunn 2002

The Dissolution of The Monasteries
Joyce Youngs 1971 George Allen and Unwin

The Pilgrimage of Grace Geoffrey Moorhouse 2002

The Pilgrimage of Grace R.W. Hoyle 2001 O.U.P.
These two books, published almost simultaneously, tell the same story with great clarity. And if you read one you will want to read the other.

From Trackways to Motorways Hugh Davies 2006 Tempus

Roads and Turnpike Trusts in Eastern Yorkshire K.A.Macmahon 1964

The Open Fields Alan Harris 1959
These are both publications of the East Yorkshire Local History Society.

The Yorkshire Hearth Tax Returns J.D.Purdy 1991 Univ.Hull

Archbishop Drummond's Visitation Returns
Borthwick Papers, 21, 23, 26

Fimber Fimber Millenium Group 2001

The History of Driffield Stephen Harrison 2002

A Time to Reap Stephen Harrison 2006
A Celebration of East Yorkshire's Agricultural History.

Of course, this list could be much longer, but all these (well, nearly all) are readable and most are accessible (perhaps with a little gentle prodding) from your local library.

Reading the Wetwang Saga could lead you into a lifetime of enjoyable reading and study.